Into the Realm of Oberon

Springer
New York
Berlin
Heidelberg
Barcelona
Budapest
Hong Kong
London
Milan
Paris
Santa Clara
Singapore
Tokyo

Eric Nikitin

Into the Realm of Oberon

An Introduction to Programming and
the Oberon-2 Programming Language

 Springer

Eric Nikitin
Bell & Howell Publication Systems Company
Kinross Lakes
Richfield, Ohio 44286
USA

Library of Congress Cataloging-in-Publication Data
Nikitin, Eric W.
    Into the realm of Oberon : an introduction to programming and the
    Oberon-2 programming language / Eric W. Nikitin.
        p.   cm.
    ISBN 0-387-98279-5 (hc : alk. paper)
    1. Object-oriented programming (Computer science)   2. Operating
systems (Computers)   3. Oberon.
QA76.64.N55   1997
005.13′3 — dc21   97-22886

Printed on acid-free paper.

Production managed by Timothy Taylor; manufacturing supervised by Jacqui Ashri.
Photocomposed copy prepared using the author's Microsoft Word files.
Printed and bound by Hamilton Printing Co., Rensselaer, NY.
Printed in the United States of America.

9 8 7 6 5 4 3 2 1

ISBN 0-387-98279-5 Springer-Verlag New York Berlin Heidelberg   SPIN 10633114

In memory of my father,
Mitchell Nikitin

For supplemental files relating to this book, go to the Springer New York Web site at:
http://www.springer-ny.com/supplements/nikitin.

Acknowledgments

This book would not have been possible without my "standing on the shoulders of giants." I would like to thank those who provided both technical inspiration and moral support:

Professor Niklaus Wirth, whose contributions to the field of computer programming are too numerous to mention, and without whom the programming language Oberon as we know it would not exist.

Professor Hanspeter Mössenböck for his work on Oberon-2.

All the contributors in the Oberon newsgroup, comp.lang.oberon, for answers and clarifications I could find nowhere else.

Martin Gilchrist at Springer-Verlag for seeing the value of publishing this book.

Scott, Hanna, Frank, Erika, Dawnette, and Cathie for giving me confidence when I needed it most.

My children, Alexander, Christopher, Katharine, and Spenser, who are my life.

And special thanks to my wife, Tammy.

Akron, Ohio   Eric Nikitin

Contents

Introduction

i.1   Who Should Use This Book?

Despite all that has been written about *programming languages*, there seems to be a noticeable weakness—a scarcity of good material for beginners. Beginners could be those who would like to learn how to program, but have never done it before. Or beginners could be those new to a particular programming language.

Many programming language books and tutorials seem to assume that the reader has some prior experience, or that there is some sort of instructor present who can explain all the details that the tutorial leaves out.

This book, however, is written with the intention of making the learning experience for novices as painless as possible. I have tried to keep my assumptions about prior knowledge to a minimum—although, as with anything, some assumptions need to be made. I do assume that the reader has minimal knowledge about how to use a computer (typing in text, selecting menu items—that sort of thing).

This book is not just for those who have never programmed, but also for programmers new to the Algol/Pascal "family" of languages. Since many general concepts are foreign to those fluent in other programming languages, and problems are often approached in a different manner, even experienced programmers might want a basic and straightforward explanation of language structures.

Finally, this book is also written for any programmer who just wants to learn the programming language Oberon-2 (subsequently referred to as Oberon). Despite the fact that most people who know Pascal or Modula-2 should have no trouble switching to Oberon, there are those who may want the features of the language explained in informal, simple terms.

Whether you are a novice or an expert, you will find some benefit to this book.

i.2   What Is Programming?

Computers are not as intelligent as some people might lead you to believe. In fact, one could even say that computers are stupid; they are no more intelligent than a toaster or an automobile. The only reason that computers *seem* intelligent is because people have written **software**—computer programs—that performs intelligently.

Programs are instructions that a computer will follow. The basic instructions that a computer can "understand" are not much more complicated than what can be done with a hand-held calculator. When large numbers of these instructions are put together, however, the computer can do many impressive things—from figuring out your taxes to computer animation to guiding a spacecraft in its proper orbit.

The basic "language" of a computer—called *machine language* or *machine code*—consists of *bits* (binary digits, 0 or 1) and *bytes* (groupings of bits). Machine language is very difficult for human beings to read and write, even though it's "natural" for the computer.

A multitude of programming languages have been created so that human beings would have an easier time writing software. The programmer writes *source text* in a programming language, which is then translated by a special program called a *compiler* or *interpreter* into machine language instructions that the computer executes.

These days, programming seems to have become a bad word. People don't want to be *programmers* anymore—they want to be *analysts* or s*oftware designers*. But programming is as important (if not more important) as analysis and design. No matter how thorough the analysis of the problem or how well designed the software, without good programming practices, the software will not run correctly.

The choice of programming language is also often discounted these days. Someone might say, "If you have a good design, it won't matter what programming language is used." I disagree; programming languages have a profound effect on how we approach a programming problem.

i.3   Why Oberon?

Oberon is a direct descendant of the programming languages Pascal and Modula-2. Pascal is still in wide use at many universities for teaching programming. However, it is slowly being subsumed by more "marketable" programming languages.

The original Pascal language is dated and was never truly intended to be more than a teaching tool. As a result, *compiler* vendors "extended" the Pascal language. Most languages calling themselves Pascal are really no closer to the original Pascal than any other existing programming language.

Oberon, however, has been built on its family heritage. Oberon proceeds directly from its predecessors; that is, it combines their best features with a few important new concepts.

Oberon is very similar to its direct predecessor Modula-2. Oberon's inventors stripped Modula-2 of features they felt did not greatly contribute to its expressiveness, making Oberon a simpler language. It is not, however, just a collection of unrelated language features. It has been consistently designed with simplicity as a primary goal.

The Oberon language provides program safety, modularity, readability, maintainability, efficiency, and support for *programming-in-the-large*. And yet it attempts to be "as simple as possible." This does *not* mean that Oberon is any less powerful (entire operating systems have been written in Oberon). What it does mean is that Oberon is less daunting to learn, yet still scales well from simple programming tasks to programming-in-the-large.

It is my contention that Oberon is an excellent language for teaching good programming practices. Oberon supports many different programming styles and methods. Once a firm foundation has been laid, those programming practices and methods can then be applied to learning other programming languages. Professional programmers *should* be familiar with a number of different programming languages.

i.4   Where to Begin

There are a large number of Oberon compilers and development environments available both commercially and for educational purposes.

Once you have acquired an Oberon compiler, you will need to read the documentation that comes with it in order to find out how to compile and execute programs. Each compiler is different, but the Oberon compilers that I have used have been relatively easy to learn to use.

After you have gotten the compiler, figure out how to type in source text and compile it. Then you are ready to start programming.

This book has 3 major divisions: Procedures, Types, and Type-bound Procedures. It is recommended to the novice to follow these divisions in order; experienced programmers may want to skip around.

Procedures are the major building blocks for telling the computer what you want to do. Procedures describe the actions the computer is to perform. That is, they are basically a list or block of instructions that the programmer wishes the computer to follow. Procedures help us break programming problems down to smaller, more easily solved pieces.

Types are descriptions of the data or information that the computer works with when following the instructions we have described in procedures.

Type-bound procedures combine procedures with types to create a very powerful way of solving computer problems.

And now, into the realm of Oberon ...

Part I

Procedures

Chapter 1
Using Procedures

1.1   A First Program

As stated in the introduction, **procedures** are a list or block of instructions or statements that the programmer wishes the computer to follow. A programmer uses procedures to solve problems and get the computer to perform actions. Procedures can be used as general-purpose routines and are often given **arguments**—values that change with each procedure call.

Let us take a look at an Oberon "program" before we get too bogged down in terminology,

```
MODULE OfeHello;

    IMPORT Out;

    PROCEDURE Do*;
    BEGIN
        Out.String("Hello World"); Out.Ln
    END Do;

END OfeHello.
```

Try typing this source text *exactly* as it appears here into your computer (make sure you pay attention to capitalization), and then compile it. You will have to read the documentation that comes with your compiler to find out exactly how to do this (generally this is a fairly easy thing to do—all I have to do for my compiler is highlight the source text and make a selection `compile` from a development menu).

If you have made a mistake in typing in the source text, you may get some **compiler errors**—mistakes in the source text that the compiler notifies you about. If this happens, try to fix the source text, and then compile it again.

Running programs in Oberon is actually just telling the system to run a procedure like `Do` in the above example. Such executable procedures are called **commands**. You can execute the command `OfeHello.Do` (again, see the documentation that comes with your compiler for how to do this—I just have to highlight the command and select a menu item `execute`).

In most Oberon environments, `OfeHello.Do` will write the words

`Hello World`

to a special place called the *system log*. The **system log,** or simply the **log**, is a listing of what goes on in your environment. You will see compiler messages in the log, for instance. There are other ways of writing out text from an Oberon program, but we won't look at them in this book because they are **implementation dependent**—different for each compiler. If you run your Oberon program in an environment that doesn't provide a system log, it should still write the words "Hello World" someplace, but you may have to read the documentation to determine where that might be.

Let's take a closer look at OfeHello:

`MODULE OfeHello;`

The first line consists of the word MODULE (notice it's in all upper-case letters), and the name OfeHello followed by a semicolon. Oberon programs are organized into individual pieces called *modules*. Modules help programmers to structure and organize procedures (as well as other things, as we'll see later on).

MODULE is an Oberon **keyword**—a word Oberon reserves for a particular use. In this case, MODULE lets us give this particular module a name, which happens to be OfeHello. That name is used for executing commands and for *importing* into other modules.

The semicolon is used as a **statement separator**—a way for the compiler to distinguish between one statement and the next.

Statements are the basic units of activity in Oberon; a statement specifies an action. A sequence of actions is then called a **statement sequence**. There are many kinds of statements; just remember that, in general, statements need to be separated by semicolons.

`IMPORT Out;`

This next line (again, notice the word IMPORT is in all capital letters) will let us use procedures that have already been written in other modules. Your Oberon compiler comes with a *library module* called `Out`, which contains procedures for writing to the system log.

Module libraries are extremely important to programmers. We don't want to have to start from scratch every time we write a new program, so we import modules written by other programmers, or other modules we have written ourselves, in order to get the most use—and reuse—out of the source text we write. We'll discuss the concept of programming for reuse more as we go along.

At this point, just remember that you need to import a module before you can use its procedures. The IMPORT statement tells the compiler which modules you're going to use.

`PROCEDURE Do*;`

This line is a *procedure declaration*, which gives the procedure a name—in this case we have named it Do. Procedures must be declared, and this **declaration** consists of a *procedure heading* and a *procedure body*.

We need the asterisk to tell the compiler that we wish to *export* this procedure. When a procedure is exported, it is made available for use outside of the module where it is declared. For instance, we couldn't issue the command `OfeHello.Do` unless the procedure `Do` had been exported from module OfeHello. The asterisk, in this situation, is called an **export mark**.

`BEGIN`

The keyword BEGIN tells the compiler where the *procedure body* starts. There is no semicolon needed after BEGIN.

`Out.String("Hello World"); Out.Ln`

Here is where the real action takes place; these are the statements that will be performed when the command is executed. Recall that we imported module Out; the Out in Out.String and Out.Ln refer back to the module Out. This means that when someone wrote module Out, they wrote a procedure String and a procedure Ln, which were exported. Now we can use those procedures without having to write them ourselves.

When we write `Out.String("Hello World")` in the source text, we are making a **procedure call**—invoking or activating the named procedure.

To call an *imported procedure*, you have to use the module name followed by a period and then the procedure name, for example,

`moduleName.procedureName`

This lets us tie procedures and modules together—you always know exactly which module provided the procedure. In this case, the module name is called a **qualified identifier**—the association of one name with another; the procedure name is always associated with the module name.

The library of a given system may contain a large number of modules. We don't need to see them all at once. The import list and qualified identifiers provide a way to avoid *naming conflicts*—I can give my procedure the same name that has already been used in another module.

Let us look closer at the procedures Out.String and Out.Ln.

Notice that Out.String has an **argument**—a value that can be changed each time we make a procedure call. Arguments to procedures are enclosed in parentheses. The argument is given or *passed* to Out.String and the procedure does the actual work of writing "Hello World" to the system log. We could have written just about anything we wanted between the double quotes—`Out.String("I love you")`, for instance—as long as it fits on a single line.

The `"I love you"` is referred to as a **literal string**—literal because we mean to use it exactly as we typed it in, and once we've compiled it, we can't change its value. The term **string** means a sequence of *characters*. **Characters** are simply the letters, numbers, and symbols that you can type on your computer keyboard.

Out.Ln is **parameterless**, meaning it has no arguments. Out.Ln writes a special character called a *newline* to the system log. **Newline** provides a way to simulate pressing the

<ENTER> key on your keyboard, permitting us to go to a "new line" when writing out text to the log.

You may be wondering why there is no semicolon after Out.Ln. The reason is that the very next statement, END, is a keyword—it's actually the same reason why we didn't need a semicolon after BEGIN. Keywords *delimit statements*; that is, they separate or mark boundaries between them, which is exactly what semicolons are supposed to do.

However, you *could* have put semicolons after BEGIN and after Out.Ln; it wouldn't have changed the meaning of the procedure. But the extra semicolons would have been interpreted by the compiler as **empty statements**—statements that contain no actions to perform. As a matter of style, we try to leave out extra semicolons.

```
END Do;
```

This marks the end of the procedure. It helps the compiler and human readers of the program know where the procedure ends.

```
END OfeHello.
```

Just as we marked the end of the procedure, we also mark the end of the module. Notice that a period is required here after the module name.

1.2   Pausing for a Moment

If you are new to programming, you may want to take at least a short break at this point. The previous section introduced a lot of terminology, and it may seem a bit overwhelming. Don't worry if you haven't memorized all the new terms. The important thing is to begin to get an understanding of the different parts that make up an Oberon program. Go back and review if you need to do so.

You may be wondering to yourself, "Why did we have to write so much source text just to get one line written out to the system log? Couldn't they have made it easier to do than that?"

The answer is yes, it could have been made easier to write out a single line of text. For such a simple program, we *are* doing extra work. But our main goal isn't to write simple programs. We want to be able to write things like tax software or computer animation software. As our programs get more complicated, we want to be able to break them up into smaller pieces—modules and procedures—that we are able to understand more easily. We have to accept that our simple programs are made a little more complicated so that our complicated programs can be made much simpler.

As you may have guessed, "programs" in Oberon are made up of modules. There is no "main program" that is executed; the procedure is the **executable unit**. Procedures, in the form of commands, can be run just as we did with Hello.Do.

In OfeHello, our program actually consisted of two modules—the one we wrote (OfeHello) and the one we imported (Out).

Modules, in turn, are made up of procedures and other things that we'll learn about
later. In our first program, we wrote one procedure ourselves, Do. And yet we used two
other procedures, Out.String and Out.Ln, which were written by someone else.

1.3   Identifiers and Reserved Words

Modules and procedures need to be named, that is, given *identifiers*. An **identifier** is a
word that is defined or declared by the programmer to be used as a name within a program. In Oberon, identifiers must begin with a letter and then be followed by a sequence
of letters and digits. Identifiers can't have spaces, hyphens, underscores or any other special characters. So,

```
x       Scan        Oberon2    C3P0  myVeryOwnIdentifier
```

are all valid identifiers, but

```
123y                (* begins with an number *)
An_Id               (* contains an underscore *)
a$badIdentifier     (* contains a '$' *)
```

would all be invalid for the reason indicated.

Oberon is **case sensitive,** which means that capitalization matters, so be careful when
typing in names. For example,

```
    name        Name        NAME
```

would all be considered different identifiers.

There are certain words that you are not allowed to use as identifiers:

ARRAY	END	MODULE	THEN
BEGIN	EXIT	NIL	TO
BY	FOR	OF	TYPE
CASE	IF	OR	UNTIL
CONST	IMPORT	POINTER	VAR
DIV	IN	PROCEDURE	WHILE
DO	IS	RECORD	WITH
ELSE	LOOP	REPEAT	
ELSIF	MOD	RETURN	

These are called *keywords* or **reserved words**—words reserved by Oberon as its
"basic vocabulary," and these words may *not* be redefined. That is, you can't use reserved words as identifiers.

Is End a reserved word? No. Remember that reserved words in Oberon are in all
capital letters. So, END is a reserved word, not End.

1.4   Comments

By the way, there is something very important that we left out of OfeHello, something that should appear in every module that you write—*comments*. **Comments** are written by the programmer to help clarify what is happening within the module.

As far as the compiler is concerned, however, comments are unnecessary. In fact, the compiler ignores comments completely. Everything within (* ... *) is ignored (except for another '(*'). Such as,

```
(* This is an example comment *)
```

Or

```
(* This is one comment (* nested inside *) another *)
```

As the example shows, you may have one comment within another; this is called **nesting**. Nested comments allow a somewhat useful "programmer's trick" to be used to hide or *comment out* a section of source text that already has comments. That is, place a part of your source text inside a comment so that the compiler ignores it.

```
Out.String( "This part prints." ); Out.Ln;
(* Out.String( "This part is commented out." );
   Out.String( "It won't print." ); *)
Out.String( "This prints too." ); Out.Ln;
```

The preceding program fragment would write the following to the log,

```
This part prints.
This prints too.
```

You should be careful when using this trick; recall that everything inside the pair (* *) is ignored by the compiler except for another '(*'. For example,

```
(* Out.String( "(* starts another comment." ); *)
```

would cause a compiler error. The compiler identifies the second '(*' as the start of a nested comment; and we have not provided a second '*)' to end it. There are safer ways to test programs—and hide parts of the source text. I will discuss some simple *debugging* strategies as the book progresses.

1.5   "Bugs"

You may have heard the term *bug* or buggy when people talk about programs that aren't working properly. A **bug** is really some sort of error in the software. Bugs don't just appear out of nowhere—programmers put them in as they write the source text. That is, the programmers made mistakes.

Some people don't like the use of the word "bug" because it seems to imply that the bug got in there by itself. Those people might rather use one the terms "program error" or "programmer error."

I don't have a problem using the word bug, and I'll continue to use it in this book. I'll just qualify it by repeating that programmers put bugs into programs—they don't just "crawl in there" by themselves.

There are two kinds of bugs: *syntactic* and *semantic*.

Syntactic bugs are language errors—the programmer has not used the Oberon language properly. Misspelling a reserved word or forgetting a semicolon are examples of syntactic bugs. This sort of bug is often found by the compiler as you compile your source text.

Semantic bugs are logic errors and are harder to find. When the programmer wrote the source text, it compiled fine. But for some reason, it doesn't do what the programmer intended. The program might **crash** (stop running and produce a *trap)* or it may just not do what it is supposed to do. You want to be very careful when writing your programs that they do what you intend them to do. Taking time to design your program before you start writing source text is a good way to accomplish this.

A word about traps; a **trap** represents the state of the program when it ends abnormally. Most Oberon systems produce traps when a program crashes. In other words, the program has encountered a **fatal run-time error**—a bug that occurs while a program is running that is severe enough to stop the program's execution. The trap—which has "trapped" the error—may simply write a message to the system log, or produce some other form of output to notify the user of the system of what has gone wrong.

As programmers you want to make programs robust enough that they never produce any traps. But in the meantime, if your program does happen to crash, a trap can provide valuable information about why it crashed. There are times when you may *want* to stop or *abort* your program and produce traps *on purpose* to help find semantic bugs. Later on, we'll examine traps in more detail and see some example output that might typically be produced and how to use it to your advantage.

1.6   Exercises

1.   Name all the different parts of an Oberon "program" that you have learned thus far.

2.   What is the purpose of a semicolon within Oberon source text?

3.   Describe the difference between a trap and the error that produced it.

4.   Describe the differences between a "program", a module, and a procedure.

5.   List the Oberon keywords that have been discussed up to this point, and describe their purposes in your own words.

Write your own modules that will perform the following:

6. Write out your name and a greeting. Make it write out both vertically and horizontally.

7. Write out a five letter palindrome in the format,

```
1 2 3 4 5
2 3 4 5 2
3 4 5 2 3
4 5 2 3 4
5 2 3 4 5
```

8. Write out

```
A B R A C A D A B R A
 A B R A C A D A B R
  A B R A C A D A B
   A B R A C A D A
    A B R A C A D
     A B R A C A
      A B R A C
       A B R A
        A B R
         A B
          A
```

9. Write out all combinations of the three letters ABC.

Chapter 2
Values and Type

2.1   Values

Let us look at another example,

```
MODULE OfeHello2;

(*   A   module   very   similar   to   OfeHello,   with   slight
     modification *)

   IMPORT Out;

   PROCEDURE Do*;
   BEGIN
      Out.String("Hello, I'm ");
      Out.Int(32, 0);    (* Here is something new *)
      Out.String(" years old."); Out.Ln

   END Do;

END OfeHello2.
```

Compile OfeHello2, and then execute the command OfeHello2.Do. You should see the following message in the log:

```
Hello, I'm 32 years old.
```

There is a procedure in this module that we haven't seen before, called Out.Int. Why do we need this new procedure? After all, we could have done

```
      Out.String("Hello, I'm 32 years old.")
```

and it would have written the same thing.

Out.String is used for *string values,* and as was said before, strings are sequences of characters. But computers are good for more than just literally repeating what we tell them; they are also good for making calculations. We need a way to represent **numeric**

values—numbers that can be used for calculations such as addition, subtraction, multiplication, and division.

The different kinds of values that Oberon "knows" how to use are as follows:

1.   A **character** is a single letter, digit, space, or punctuation mark.

2.   A **string** is a sequence of characters.

3.   Numbers are broken into *integers* and *real numbers*:

   a.   An **integer** is a whole number—positive, negative, or zero.

   5   −12   4545   0

   b.   A **real number** is what we think of as *a decimal number*— numbers that contain a decimal point.

   3.14   2.0   −162.5   0.0

4.   **Boolean** values are limited to the values TRUE and FALSE.

Note: Commas never appear in numeric values in Oberon: 1,000,000 needs to be written 1000000.

Character, integer, and boolean values are also referred to as **ordinal values**—values which come in an ordered sequence and can be counted. The number 1 is followed by 2 and so on. But because of the way real values are stored on the computer, reals are not ordinal values.

The Int in Out.Int is short for integer. Out.Int is used for writing integer values to the log. One of the advantages of using Out.Int is that we can use an *expression* as an argument. An **expression** is a part of a statement that represents a value. It generally consists of several *operands* and *operators*. For example, we could have used:

```
Out.Int(15 + 17, 0);
```

in OfeHello2 and still have gotten the same output. The expression 15 + 17 is evaluated to produce the value 32.

We cannot perform arithmetic operations such as addition directly on string values, but we *can* do so with numeric values.

Out.Int contains something else that's new: a *second* argument—the zero that appears after the comma. In Oberon, procedures can have more than one argument. Multiple arguments are separated by commas.

Why do we need a second argument in Out.Int? Because when writing out numeric values, sometimes we want to be able to control the **field width**—how much space is used when printing out the value. If we use a field width of 0 or 1, then the number takes the minimum amount of space required to display itself. In the case of OfeHello2, the number 32 requires two places when written out.

For practice, try changing OfeHello2 to use more than two places when writing out the integer value. For example,

```
Out.Int(32, 5);
```

will produce the output:

```
Hello, I'm    32 years old.
```

Notice that the output of Out.Int is **right justified,** which means spaces are padded on the left side to move the number to the right side.

Caution! In many Oberon systems, modules are **dynamically loaded**—modules are loaded into computer memory only when they're needed, and the whole program isn't necessarily loaded all at the same time. This means that after you compile your changes to OfeHello2, you may need to explicitly *unload* the old module from the first time you ran OfeHello2.Do. Otherwise, when you recompile the module and execute the command again, you won't see the effects of the changes you made.

You will have to read your system's documentation to see how to unload the old copy of OfeHello2 from memory.

2.2   String and Character Values

As you might guess, string and character values are closely related. After all, strings are made up of characters.

As was said before, string values are represented by sequences of characters surrounded by quote marks. Up to this, point, we have used double quotes (") in our modules. But single quotes (') can also be used to *delimit* literal string values. *The opening quote must be the same as the closing quote*, which is actually part of the reason why there are two ways of showing string values. For instance, you may have been wondering how to write out a double quote ("). You could use,

```
'I said, "Hello, world!"'
```

to represent a string value. If we used Out.String('I said, "Hello, world!"'), then

```
I said, "Hello, world!"
```

would be written to the log.

For consistency, you should use double quotes almost exclusively. The only exception is when you want a double quote to appear within the string, as in the above example.

Character values are represented in one of two ways. The first is based on the character's *ordinal position*. Recall that ordinal describes something that comes in an ordered sequence and can be counted; say "B" comes after "A," and so on. The ordinal position for characters in Oberon is represented as a *hexadecimal number*. We will look at hexadecimal representation in the next section.

Rather than have to deal with hexadecimal numbers, we can also represent character values as *strings with a length of one*. That is, a single character within double or single quotes.

$$\text{"a"} \qquad \text{'Z'} \qquad \text{"("} \qquad \text{'+'} \qquad \text{"\&"}$$

This works out almost as well as using a hexadecimal representation. The only disadvantage is that some of the special characters, such as a tab or newline, cannot be written as a string.

2.3   Hexadecimal Numbers

Hexadecimal numbers—or "hex" numbers—are useful because of the way computers actually store values—as *bits*. Recall that a **bit**—binary digit—can have only the values 0 or 1. It just so happens that a sequence of 4 bits (sometimes referred to as a **nibble**) can be easily represented by a hex number.

The word **hexadecimal** means that the numbering system is based on 16 "digits" rather than the 10 digits we're used to. Four bits are just the perfect size to represent numbers from 0 to 15, which is the exact range of hex digits. This fact makes hex numbers a convenient way of representing numbers on many computers.

Hex digits are the normal ones we know: 0, 1, 2, 3, 4, 5, 6, 7, 8, and 9 plus the "digits" A, B, C, D, E, and F. It can be confusing to try to think of a hex number as standing for a number or a character, and many people still need to resort to tables to translate them. To give you an idea, look at Table 2.1, which shows how to translate the numbers 0 through 15.

Notice that the numbers 0 through 9 look the same in either decimal or hex. After that, to represent a decimal "10" we use the hex number "A," decimal "11" is "B" in hex, and so on.

Just as in decimal, when we run out of digits, we start over at 0 and add another place value. That is, in decimal, 9 is followed by 10; we need two digits to represent the number 10. Similarly in hex, F is followed by 10. But remember, hex is based on 16 digits, so hex 10 is really the same as decimal 16.

The reason why characters are sometimes represented as hex numbers is because hex numbers can often be used easily to represent *bytes*. A **byte** is generally defined as the amount of space (i.e., number of bits) a particular computer uses to store a single character value. Very often, a byte is either 8 or 16 bits. On a computer that uses 8 bits for each character, we need only 2 hex digits to represent them.

Table 2.1: Hexadecimal Representation

Binary (4 bits)	Decimal	Hex (1 nibble)
0000	0	0
0001	1	1
0010	2	2
0011	3	3
0100	4	4
0101	5	5
0110	6	6
0111	7	7
1000	8	8
1001	9	9
1010	10	A
1011	11	B
1100	12	C
1101	13	D
1110	14	E
1111	15	F

Characters in Oberon are most often represented by the *ASCII* (American Standard Code for Information Interchange) *character set* (or sometimes one of the extensions to ASCII such as *Latin-1*—you should check your system documentation to verify whether it uses the ASCII character set). **ASCII** is a standard character set used by many computers and programming language implementations, and it represents a total of 128 characters.

The first 32 characters are called **control characters**—nonprinting characters that are used to control the output or input of the computer (to the screen or a printer, for example). The very last character is also a control character.

An *ASCII table* is given here to show the hex number for each character:

Table 2.2: ASCII Character Set

Dec	Hex	Char	Dec	Hex	Char	Dec	Hex	Char
0	00	^@ NUL	43	2B	+	86	56	V
1	01	^A SOH	44	2C	,	87	57	W
2	02	^B STX	45	2D	-	88	58	X
3	03	^C ETX	46	2E	.	89	59	Y
4	04	^D EOT	47	2F	/	90	5A	Z
5	05	^E ENQ	48	30	0	91	5B	[
6	06	^F ACK	49	31	1	92	5C	\
7	07	^G BEL	50	32	2	93	5D	]
8	08	^H BS	51	33	3	94	5E	^
9	09	^I HT	52	34	4	95	5F	_
10	0A	^J LF	53	35	5	96	60	`
11	0B	^K VT	54	36	6	97	61	a
12	0C	^L FF	55	37	7	98	62	b
13	0D	^M CR	56	38	8	99	63	c
14	0E	^N SO	57	39	9	100	64	d
15	0F	^O SI	58	3A	:	101	65	e
16	10	^P DLE	59	3B	;	102	66	f
17	11	^Q DC1	60	3C	<	103	67	g
18	12	^R DC2	61	3D	=	104	68	h
19	13	^S DC3	62	3E	>	105	69	i
20	14	^T DC4	63	3F	?	106	6A	j
21	15	^U NAK	64	40	@	107	6B	k
22	16	^V SYN	65	41	A	108	6C	l
23	17	^W ETB	66	42	B	109	6D	m
24	18	^X CAN	67	43	C	110	6E	n
25	19	^Y EM	68	44	D	111	6F	o
26	1A	^Z SUB	69	45	E	112	70	p
27	1B	^[ESC	70	46	F	113	71	q
28	1C	^\ FS	71	47	G	114	72	r
29	1D	^] GS	72	48	H	115	73	s
30	1E	^^ RS	73	49	I	116	74	t
31	1F	^_ US	74	4A	J	117	75	u
32	20		75	4B	K	118	76	v
33	21	!	76	4C	L	119	77	w
34	22	"	77	4D	M	120	78	x
35	23	#	78	4E	N	121	79	y
36	24	$	79	4F	O	122	7A	z
37	25	%	80	50	P	123	7B	{
38	26	&	81	51	Q	124	7C	|
39	27	'	82	52	R	125	7D	}
40	28	(	83	53	S	126	7E	~
41	29	)	84	54	T	127	7F	DEL
42	2A	*	85	55	U			

2.4 Character and Integer Values as Hex Numbers

As the ASCII table in the last section should illustrate, both character values and integer values can be represented as hex numbers. Refer back to the ASCII table to help see how this works.

In Oberon, character values use the letter 'X' when represented in hex. That is, the hex number is followed by an 'X' (Note that there are no quotes around the hex number, in contrast to when you represent a character as a string),

```
The letter "N" is 4EX
The "escape character" is 1BX
A "tab character" is 09X
The letter "x" is 78X
```

In Oberon, integer values use the letter 'H' when represented in hex. The hex value is followed by an 'H':

```
Decimal 15 is 0FH in hex
Decimal 42 is 2AH in hex
Decimal 120 is 78H in hex
Decimal 127 is 7FH in hex
```

Why would we want to use hex representations?

For characters, there are times when you need to be able to access *nonprintable* characters, like a tab for instance. Hex values give us a way around the restrictions of what we are able to type on the keyboard. Also, if your Oberon system uses a non-ASCII character set, you may need to represent some other kinds of special characters as hex numbers.

For integers, hex representation can help when you're interfacing with programs or libraries written in other programming languages or when doing **low-level programming**—writing programs that interact closely with computer hardware.

2.5 Reals and Floating-point Notation

Real values can be represented as *decimal numbers* (always without commas) as we have seen already. However, they can also be represented in *floating-point notation*. **Floating-point notation** is very similar to *scientific notation* in that the number is represented as a decimal number times a power of 10. We use the letter 'E' (or sometimes 'D', as we shall see a little later), which stands for "times ten to the power of" and is followed by an integer number referred to as the **scale factor**.

```
4.567E8    equals 4.567 times 10 to the 8th power
           or 456700000
```

```
9.0E4     equals 9.0 times 10 to the 4^th power
          or 90000
0.577E-7  equals 0.577 times 10 to the negative
          7^th power or 0.0000000577
```

In Oberon, real numbers must always contain a decimal point. Also, there must always be a digit in front of the decimal point—even if that digit is zero. So you couldn't write 0.5 as .5 or you would get compile-time errors.

2.6   Boolean Values

Boolean values can be one of only two things, TRUE or FALSE. As you learn more about programming, you will see that it is often to our advantage to be able to test *conditions*—to check whether a condition is true or false. For instance, when writing procedures it is often necessary to make decisions as to what course of action to follow. Boolean values are used to express the state of these kinds of decisions.
We will talk more about boolean values in later chapters.

2.7   Exercises

1. Name the different kinds of values that can be represented in Oberon and give examples of situations when you might want to use each kind.

2. What kind of value is each of the following (note that there may be more than one answer for each):

    a. 117   f. FFX
    b. 24.0   g. "FFX"
    c. 9111234   h. EEH
    d. "4"   i. 'EEH'
    e. "13464"   j. 1AFH

3. Convert the following hex values to decimal:

    a. 25   c. 36
    b. 5D   d. 6A

4. Convert the following decimal values to hex:

    a. 25   c. 63
    b. 51   d. 117

5. Write the following real values in floating-point notation:

   a. 1745.0   c. 63050000000.0
   b. 0.75   d. 0.000000066778

6. Write the following in decimal notation:

   a. 7.649E-01   c. 1.114252E-08
   b. 3.67E+02   d. 8.72529E+10

7. Write a module in which you use Out.Int to write out a table of numbers so that all values are right justified. Each column in your table should have some appropriate heading. For example,

   ```
   SEQUENCE   PART NUMBER    TOTAL
   --------   -----------    -----
       25       123456789    500
      174      98765432100    35
   ```

8. Can you use Out.String to write out character values? What about character values in hex notation? Why or why not? Write a module to test this.

Chapter 3
Writing Procedures

3.1   Procedures with Parameters

Let us look at an example involving writing a procedure that has parameters:

```
MODULE OfeInitials;

(* Used to output several sets of initials to the log *)

   IMPORT Out;

   PROCEDURE WriteInitials(first, last: CHAR);
   (* This  is  the  first  procedure  we've  written  that
      has parameters *)
   BEGIN
      Out.Char(first);
      Out.Char(last);
      Out.Ln
   END WriteInitials;

   PROCEDURE Do*;
   (* Calls the same procedure three times *)
   BEGIN
      WriteInitials("E", "N");
      WriteInitials("N", "W");
      WriteInitials("T", "P")
   END Do;

END OfeInitials.
```

Can you guess what will happen if we run the command OfeInitials.Do? Try to figure it out before you compile the above module, and then actually run the command OfeInitials.Do.

When OfeInitials.Do is executed, it calls the procedure WriteInitials three times, each time with different arguments. Notice that we don't need to write `OfeInitials.WriteInitials` because the procedure WriteInitials is called from within the module where it's declared. *Only imported procedures need to be qualified with the module name.*

There are several differences of note between WriteInitials and Do. First of all, Do is exported (notice the '`*`'—the *export mark*—next to the procedure name), whereas WriteInitials isn't exported. This means that Do can be used from outside of the module—executed as a command for instance. WriteInitials can be used only within module OfeInitials.

The second difference is that we've given WriteInitials a **parameter list**—a list of named values that are to be *passed* to the procedure as arguments. During a procedure call, the values represented by the arguments (sometimes called **actual parameters**) can then be used within the called procedure.

`WriteInitials("E", "N")` does something a little different than `WriteInitials("N", "W")`.

This is exactly the way Out.String is able to write different strings to the log. We can write "Hello World" or any other string without having to *change the procedure itself*. The procedure can be used *over and over* again to do slightly different things just by changing the arguments we give it.

3.2   Parameters and the Parameter List

The use of parameters and arguments allows a different value to be used each time a procedure is called. But there are limitations on the type of arguments that the procedure will accept. If we expect an integer to be passed, we don't want to allow a string to be used as an argument. Numbers behave differently than strings; so we want to make certain that we get numbers when we expect numbers.

Each parameter (sometimes called **formal parameters**) declared in the parameter list must have two things: an *identifier* and a *type*. The notion of type is very important in Oberon, and we will examine it more in the next section.

The type of parameters that WriteInitials expects is CHAR, meaning that it expects to get single characters. In this case, there are two parameters, which are named by the programmer `first` and `last`, so when we make a procedure call to WriteInitials, two characters are *always* required for its arguments. The arguments are separated by commas.

Parameters are **positional**—the order in which they appear in the parameter list corresponds directly to the way the arguments must appear in the procedure call. In `WriteInitials("E", "N")` the "E" is associated with `first` and "N" is associated with `last`.

The identifier can then be used *within* the procedure in place of the value it represents.

You have to make sure you have the *exact* same number of arguments as there are parameters. Otherwise, you'll get a compile-time error. For example, the procedure call `WriteInitials("E")` would cause an such an error.

As long as the parameters are declared with the same type, the type needs to appear only once in the list, with each identifier separated by a comma. Or if you wish, you can write each identifier and type separately. In that case, each is separated by a semicolon. That is,

```
PROCEDURE WriteInitials(first, last: CHAR);
```

works out to be the same as:

```
PROCEDURE WriteInitials(first: CHAR; last: CHAR);
```

3.3   Basic Types

Oberon is what is known as a **strongly typed language**—all values have a specific type associated with them. This makes sense because you don't want to use a character value when you mean to use an integer. The basic types recognized by Oberon correspond for the most part to the values we have talked about already. These basic types are closely associated with how values are stored on the computer. The following is a list of basic types:

- BOOLEAN   the truth values TRUE and FALSE
- CHAR   the characters of the ASCII set (0X .. 0FFX)
- SHORTINT   the integers between −128 .. 127
- INTEGER   the integers between −32768 .. 32767
- LONGINT   the integers between −2147483648 .. 2147483647
- REAL   the real numbers between MIN(REAL) and
                                MAX(REAL): −3.4E+38 .. 3.4E+38
- LONGREAL   the real numbers between MIN(LONGREAL) and
                                MAX(LONGREAL): −1.8D+308 .. 1.8D+308
- SET   the sets of integers between 0 .. 31

Note: The ranges for values on your system might not be exactly the same for these types—these are just some typical values for them.

Let us discuss these basic types further.

Why are there three different kinds of integers and two kinds of reals? The reason has to do with the ranges indicated and how numbers are represented on computers. The bigger the numbers, the more space required in computer memory to store them. The speed at which calculations are performed could possibly be affected by the size difference as well, although this is not always the case.

We will generally use INTEGER, LONGINT, and REAL types for examples that require numeric types. Our main concern is whether the numeric type is large enough to hold the numbers we are to use—we can't use INTEGER when we need to use a value of, say, 1000000 (assuming a system that had ranges as given above)—we would have to use LONGINT instead.

For the purposes of this book, however, we won't worry about how the choice of numeric type affects speed of calculation.

One other note about real values: Notice that the range for REAL was expressed using 'E':

```
-3.4E+38 .. 3.4E+38
```

whereas LONGINT was expressed using 'D':

```
-1.8D+308 .. 1.8D+308.
```

When using floating-point notation, real values written with an 'E' are interpreted as having type REAL, and those written with a 'D' as having type LONGREAL.

The SET type will be discussed in a later chapter.

You may have noticed that there is no string type to correspond with string values. Recall that strings are defined as sequences of characters. So, the *type of a string value* is **ARRAY OF CHAR.** Here ARRAY means just what we have described—a sequence of values. We will also talk about arrays in more detail later.

3.4   Why Do We Need Types?

Representing values as a particular type helps us in a number of ways. It allows the compiler to check for certain kinds of errors that we might not otherwise find very easily. It's like the idea "a place for everything and everything in its place." Types prevent us from doing something stupid like trying to multiply character values together as if they were numbers.

Also, different types are stored differently in the computer's memory. By being explicit about types, we can be more efficient as to how we use computer resources.

3.5   MODULE Definitions

The definition of the module Out follows:

```
DEFINITION Out;

    PROCEDURE Open;
    PROCEDURE Char (ch: CHAR);
    PROCEDURE Ln;
```

```
PROCEDURE Int (VAR i, n: LONGINT);
PROCEDURE Real (x: REAL; n: INTEGER);
PROCEDURE String (s: ARRAY OF CHAR);
```

END Out.

The text between the words "DEFINITION" and "END" is termed a **definition module**—a list of all exported declarations; it is also known as the *interface* of the module.

In Oberon, module definitions are *generated*. That is, normally when a module is compiled, the compiler will create something called a *symbol file*. The symbol file serves two main purposes.

First, it is used when we have IMPORT statements in our programs. The compiler looks at the symbol files of the imported modules and checks to make sure they are used correctly. This is how the compiler checks whether the imported procedures were called with appropriate arguments, for instance.

The other purpose of the symbol files is to help programmers who want to use a module that has been imported. Oberon implementations come with something called a **browser,** which lets us look at the module definition. The browser that came with my compiler generated the above definition for module Out.

Module definitions help us as programmers to see what *operations* the module provides without having to worry about extra details. In other words, we see the *interface* and not the *implementation*.

An **interface** is the part that a user has to deal with in order to use something—the interface to a clock, for example, is the clock face (how you tell the time), some way to set the time (a knob or button on the clock), or other similar things. The **implementation** is the insides of the clock, cogs, springs and gears—or even electronic parts as in most modern clocks. As a user of a clock, I don't ever have to look at its insides in order to be able to use it.

As you look at the definition of Out, pay special attention to what lies between the parentheses in each procedure declaration. The information between each set of parentheses is the parameter list. Recall that this is a list of the expected arguments for each procedure. Notice that each parameter in the parameter list is separated by a comma or semicolon and is made up of an identifier, followed by a colon, and a type name. We shall see exactly why we need all this information very soon, but before we move on, let us take a closer look at the procedures defined in Out.

Out.Open opens the system log if it is not already opened. We normally don't have to call Out.Open because the log is usually opened automatically.

Out.Char writes out a single character value to the log.

```
Out.Char("A");
```

Out.Ln writes a newline (sometimes called a carriage return) to the log.

Out.Int writes out a LONGINT value to the log. It can actually be used to write out all of our integer types—SHORTINT, INTEGER, and LONGINT.

```
Out.Int(50, 1);
```

Out.Real writes out REAL values to the log. (Note: you can't write LONGREAL values using Out.Real.)

```
Out.Real(2.34, 0); Out.Real(6.23E-2, 9);
```

Out.String writes a string value to the log. We have seen several examples of this already.

```
Out.String("Just a string.");
```

3.6   Type Compatibility of Basic Types

For the most part, the basic types are *incompatible*. That is, you can't use one type in place of another. For example, you can't use a character where you mean to use an integer. Out.Int("5", 0) would produce a compile-time error.

However, there are times when types are compatible with one another. This is the case for numeric types. The numeric types form a kind of hierarchy; that is, a larger type *includes* the values of a smaller type:

```
LONGREAL  >=  REAL  >=  LONGINT  >=  INTEGER  >=  SHORTINT
```

What this means is that when an INTEGER is expected, a SHORTINT will work just as well. When a LONGREAL is expected, any other numeric type can be used. For example, Out.Real(5, 0); works perfectly fine—the integer value 5 is converted to a real value *automatically* by the compiler.

In general for numeric types, the smaller type is compatible with the larger—one can be converted to the other (but not the other way around).

Warning! When using a LONGINT in place of a REAL, on many computer systems the value could be **truncated**, that is, part of the value of the number might be lost. Even though the language requires REAL to include all the values represented by LONGINT, many Oberon compilers don't necessarily enforce this rule. Most of the time, you shouldn't have to worry about it, but be aware that there may be potential problems in this one case.

3.7   Basic Arithmetic Operators

Oberon has certain built-in arithmetic operators that operate on numeric types. We can perform *addition, subtraction, multiplication,* and *division*. With them we can build *expressions*.

+	addition (or sum)
−	subtraction (or difference)
*	multiplication (or product)

```
/                    division (real quotient)
DIV                  integer quotient
MOD                  modulus
```

Addition, subtraction, and multiplication work pretty much like you would expect.

```
3 + 5 gives 8             3.14 + 9 gives 12.14
9 - 5 gives 4             23 - 40.15 gives -17.15
6 * 2 gives 12            0.25 * 50 gives 12.5
```

Division, however, can be done in several ways. For instance,

```
8 divided by 5 could be 1.6
```

or

```
8 divided by 5 could be 1 with a remainder of 3
```

The first way is called *real division*; the result is a REAL (or LONGREAL) even if the operands divide out evenly. The operator "/" indicates when we want to do real division.

```
8/5 gives 1.6             7.5/1.5 gives 5.0
```

The second way to perform division is **integer division**—for this, *both* operands must be one of the integer types. We need a way to say when we want the *whole number* part of the answer or when we want the *remainder*. We use DIV to indicate when we want the whole number part and MOD when we want the remainder.

```
8 DIV 5 is 1
8 MOD 5 is 3
```

Integer division is good for problems that aren't satisfied with decimal answers. It wouldn't make sense to say, "I have 4.25 dozen eggs." You would probably want to say, "I have 4 dozen and 3 eggs."

For all of these arithmetic operators, the type of the *result* is the type of whichever operand is larger according to the hierarchy we talked about before:

```
LONGREAL  >=  REAL  >=  LONGINT  >=  INTEGER  >=  SHORTINT
```

This means basically that if you add an INTEGER and a REAL, the result would be a REAL. If you subtract a REAL from a LONGREAL, the result would be a LONGREAL. So, the numeric types can be *freely mixed in arithmetic expressions*.

When an operator is encountered, the operand's types are checked. If necessary, the smaller type is converted to the larger type. And again, the result has the same type as the larger type.

Most of the time, these *type conversions* are handled automatically. But there are some cases where explicit type conversions are required.

There are predeclared procedures that will do these explicit conversions: ENTIER(), SHORT(), and LONG(). We shall see examples of these in the section on *predeclared procedures*.

3.8   Standard Identifiers

Oberon has a number of words that are called **standard identifiers**. These are identifiers that have been predeclared and are given a particular meaning. Examples are

- Truth values: TRUE and FALSE
- Type identifiers: BOOLEAN, INTEGER, REAL, SET, etc.
- Standard procedures: ABS(), LEN(), etc.

Standard identifiers are similar to reserved words. However, unlike reserved words, standard identifiers can be redeclared. That is, you can change their meaning. For example,

```
PROCEDURE ABS;
BEGIN
...
END ABS;
```

is perfectly valid. However, such redeclarations are discouraged. After all, Oberon is case sensitive, so if you absolutely want a procedure with the same name as a standard identifier,

```
PROCEDURE Abs;
```

should work just as well for you.

All of the following identifiers are predeclared,

ABS	FALSE	NEW
ASH	HALT	ODD
ASSERT	INC	ORD
BOOLEAN	INCL	REAL
CAP	INTEGER	SET
CHAR	LEN	SHORT
CHR	LONG	SHORTINT
COPY	LONGINT	SIZE
DEC	LONGREAL	TRUE
ENTIER	MAX	
EXCL	MIN	

3.9   Exercises

1. Write out procedure headings for procedures that have the following parameter lists (choose whatever procedure names and identifiers you like). For example, for CHAR, ARRAY OF CHAR, we could write,

    ```
    PROCEDURE Insert(c: CHAR; string: ARRAY OF CHAR);
    ```

    a. CHAR, INTEGER, ARRAY OF CHAR
    b. ARRAY OF CHAR, ARRAY OF CHAR, LONGINT
    c. REAL, INTEGER, REAL
    d. ARRAY OF CHAR, INTEGER, INTEGER
    e. REAL, REAL, REAL
    f. ARRAY OF CHAR, REAL, INTEGER, CHAR

2. Explain in your own words the difference between arguments and parameters.

3. Find out how to use the browser that came with your compiler. Then see what definitions look like for Out, OfeHello, and OfeHello2.

    Some Oberon systems have more than one browser so that you can get several different views of the definition module. Some browsers permit exported comments so that we can provide comments that are viewable in a definition module. See if your system comes with such a browser. *Note*: Exported comments have to have an extra '*' used as an export mark, so that it would look like,

    ```
    (** This is an exported comment *)
    ```

4. Write a module similar to OfeHello2 that uses all the different procedures available in module Out.

5. Try changing your module from exercise 4 so that there are mistakes in your procedure calls. For instance, use Out.Char(5) and see what happens when you compile it (note that Out.Char("5") is correct).

6. Write a module that uses all of the arithmetic operators we have discussed: +, −, *, /, DIV, and MOD. Use these operators to form expressions that are used as arguments to Out.Int and Out.Real. For example,

    ```
    Out.Real(5*6/3, 0);
    ```

    Then verify that Oberon's calculations match what you expect the answers to be. If the answers come out different from what you expect, why do you think that is?

7. Write a module that writes out several large numbers with commas in appropriate places. (*Hint*: You may have to use more than one procedure call for each number written.) For example, write out the numbers

```
    1,000,000
       13,346
5,867,453,321
```

Chapter 4
Variables and Changing Values

4.1   Variables and the Assignment Operator

As usual, we will start with an example,

```
MODULE OfeAdder;

(* Adds two numbers and outputs the answer to the log *)

    IMPORT Out;

    PROCEDURE Add(first, second: INTEGER;
                    VAR result: INTEGER);
    (* This procedure does the adding *)
    BEGIN
        result := first + second;
    END Add;

    PROCEDURE OutAnswer(answer: INTEGER);
    (* This procedure outputs the answer to the log *)
    BEGIN
        Out.String("The answer is ");
        Out.Int(answer, 0);
        Out.Ln
    END OutAnswer;

    PROCEDURE Do*;
    (* Here we've added something new! *)
        VAR sum: INTEGER;
        (* What do you think this line means? *)
    BEGIN
        Add(5, 7, sum);
        OutAnswer(sum)
```

```
    END Do;

END OfeAdder.
```

Examine module OfeAdder and try to figure out what it does. After you have looked at it, compile it, and execute OfeAdder.Do.

In procedure Do, the values 5 and 7 are passed to procedure Add, which then adds the two numbers together and *returns* the result. Finally, OutAnswer is called to print out that result. What do you think the identifier sum is used for?

The identifier sum has been defined as a **variable**—a place in computer memory that has been reserved to hold a certain type of value. The statement

```
    VAR sum: INTEGER;
```

defines the variable sum to be of type integer. The statement *allocates* enough computer memory to hold an integer value, and then allows us to access that value through the name sum. We can use sum to hold that value and let us do more than one thing with it. We can add up 5 and 7 and store the result in sum so that we can write it out later.

It is something like the MEM (memory) key on a handheld calculator, only a computer has a lot more MEM places to keep track of; so it helps if we can give *meaningful names* to those memory locations.

Parameters are actually a sort of variable too. Memory is allocated to store a value, and the name of the parameter is used to access that value. Within a procedure, both parameters and the variables that are defined for that procedure can be used in exactly the same ways.

The main difference between them is that variables are meant to be used *exclusively* within the procedure—they *"disappear"* when the procedure ends. Parameters, however, may or may not still exist after the procedure ends. Parameters are used to *pass values* "into," and in some cases "out of," procedures.

Procedure Add shows both ways that the values of a variable can be changed. First, let us examine the body of Add. It contains one statement:

```
    result := first + second;
```

The symbol we haven't seen before is the ':='. This is called the *assignment operator*. The variable on the left side "gets" or "is assigned" the value of the expression on the right side.

When Add is called with the arguments 5, 7, and sum (i.e., Add(5, 7, sum)), the parameter first takes on the value 5 and second takes on the value 7. Recall that parameters are *positional*—the arguments are passed by the corresponding position in the parameter list.

The expression first + second evaluates to '5 + 7', which gives 12. Then result *gets* the value of 12; the 12 is *assigned* to result by the assignment operator. That's how you can read the line, "result gets the value of first plus second" or "result is assigned the value of first plus second."

So how does sum get the value of result? Notice that the third parameter in the list has the word VAR in front of it. This defines the parameter as a **variable parameter**—

the parameter (and also the value of the corresponding variable used as an argument) *can be changed*.

When sum is passed to Add via the call Add(5, 7, sum), result refers *directly* to sum. That is, they both *name the same stored value*. You can think of them as *aliases* for the same memory location. When we change result using the assignment operator, the value of sum is *actually changed* as well.

The other parameters—first and second—are the kind of parameters we have already discussed. They are known also as **value parameters**, meaning that *only* the value is passed.

We have talked about several new concepts here. To make sure you understand these ideas, let us take a closer look at them.

4.2   Variables

We have already said that a variable is a place in computer memory that has been reserved to hold a certain type of value.

A variable must be **defined**—an identifier is *bound* to the variable. The variable itself has two properties: its type and a value. The type of the variable specifies which values the variable may have, as well as what operations apply to it. A formal way to describe this relationship is to say that a variable is an *instance of its type*.

To define a variable, the format is,

```
VAR <variable name>: <Type>;
```

The reserved word VAR must be used when defining variables. Variables are defined after the procedure heading, but before the reserved word BEGIN. The word VAR needs to appear only once no matter how many variables are defined for that procedure. VAR is followed by a list of comma-separated identifiers, which is in turn followed by a colon and the type name. Semicolons are used to separate distinct types.

```
VAR    number, tempNumber: INTEGER;
       ch, tempCh: CHAR;
       realNumber: REAL;
(* defines two INTEGERs (number and tempNumber), two CHARs
   (ch and tempCh), and a REAL (realNumber) *)
```

The value of a variable is *undefined* until it is **initialized**—that is, given a starting value. We don't know what value the variable has until we assign a value to it. It *has* a value, but we aren't sure what it is. Values are assigned to variables using an assignment statement.

Remember, a variable should always be given a starting value. You should make it a habit to properly initialize variables in your programs before you use them.

4.3   Assignment Statements

An assignment statement changes the value of a variable. It can give the variable a starting value or alter its current value. The general form is

```
<variable> := <expression representing a value>
```

Assignment can be read as "gets," "becomes," or "is assigned."

Variables may be assigned only values of compatible types. If an incompatible value is assigned, the compiler will generate an error called a **type clash**—a mismatch of types. Most of the time, this means the types must be identical. There are some cases where the types don't have to be identical, such as numeric types; but even then, they *must* be compatible.

Here are some additional examples, which are all legal assignments:

```
VAR int: INTEGER; rl: REAL;
      ...
      int := 16;
      rl := 16;
      rl := int;
      rl := 16.5;
```

However,

```
      int := 16.5;
      int := rl;
```

are not legal. Integers cannot take on real values. Remember the hierarchy

```
LONGREAL  >=  REAL  >=  LONGINT  >=  INTEGER  >=  SHORTINT
```

Basically, this means that we can normally go only "one way" with assignments of numeric types. Integers can be assigned to reals, but not vice versa. However, there are ways to convert "backwards," say from a LONGINT to an INTEGER, using predeclared procedures, which we shall see later.

Recall that one of the reasons we have numeric types is to perform calculations. So when performing an assignment, we may actually be evaluating the result of some calculation on the right-hand side of the assignment expression. This result is then assigned to a variable. We saw one example like this already,

```
      result := first + second;
```

Some other examples are

```
      int1 := 12;
      int2 := 9;
      int3 := int1 + int2;
      (* after this assignment, int3 has the value 21 *)
```

```
rl1 := int1/int2;
(* legal, int1 and int2 are converted to real values
    rl1 has the value 0.75 after this assignment *)

rl2 := 5 * (int1 + int3) / 3;
(* int1 + int3 evaluates to 12 + 21 or 33, which is
multiplied times 5 and then divided by 3, the final
value of rl2 is 55.0 *)
```

Notice the use of parentheses in the above examples to help clarify which operation is to be performed first.

In any assignment, the expression on the right side is evaluated first to yield a result. The variable on the left side then gets the value of that result.

If you recall our discussion about character values, there are two ways to represent character values that may be assigned. Either as hex values

```
ch := 09X;

ch := 5FX;
```

or as string values of length one,

```
ch := "C";
ch := "6";
```

Note that the following assignments would not be valid character assignments,

```
ch := 6;
(* An integer value assigned to a CHAR variable *)

ch := C;
(* In this case, C is interpreted as a variable name.
    If C were defined as 'C: CHAR;' then this would be
    OK *)
```

4.4   String Variables and Assignments

A string variable is defined as, for example,

```
VAR string: ARRAY 10 OF CHAR;
```

The type ARRAY OF CHAR has been mentioned briefly before. String values have the type ARRAY OF CHAR.

Buy why do we need the 10 when defining the variable string? Remember, part of the reason we need to specify a type in a variable definition is to reserve a place in computer memory—to allocate the space needed to store the value the variable represents.

An array is a sequence of values. The computer has no way of knowing how many values you want to be able to store. Therefore, we have to tell it explicitly.

The 10 in the variable definition of string means that we can store up to 10 values in the array (actually, for strings, we can't store more than 9 characters because the last place is reserved for a special "string terminating" character 0X that lets us know when we have reached the end of the string). We will find out more on how to work with strings later on.

At this point, just remember that variables defined as ARRAY OF CHAR need to have the length specified. The general form to define a string variable is

```
VAR <variable name>: ARRAY <length> OF CHAR;
```

String values may be assigned to a character array. Assuming

```
VAR string: ARRAY 10 OF CHAR,
```

the assignments

```
string := "nineChars";
string := "Hi.";
string := "";
(* assigning an empty string, that is, a string with
   no characters *)

string := 41X;
(* This might seem strange, but it's the same as
   string := "A" (assuming ASCII characters) *)
```

are all legal. However, the assignments

```
string := "I'm too long";
(* ERROR! string doesn't have enough space to hold the
   value *)

string := 16;
(* ERROR! Can't assign an integer value to a string *)
```

are not legal.

4.5 Variables Versus Parameters

A procedure may have its own **local variables**—those variables defined within the procedure. A procedure may also have parameters declared in its parameter list. Let us look at how local variables and parameters interact.

At the time of the procedure call, arguments are paired with parameters based on their respective positions in the parameter list. Any arguments that are expressions are evaluated and those results are assigned to the parameters. Therefore, the expression must be *assignment compatible* with the type of the parameter.

The parameters can then be treated very much like local variables. But parameters have already been initialized by the arguments, whereas the local variables still need to be given starting values.

A variable is a place used to store a value, and is visible only within its procedure. A parameter is used to "carry" values to and from procedures, and may still exist after the procedure ends.

Every variable and parameter has a specific type associated with it. Declarations associate an identifier to that type. The variable or parameter can then be used to represent values of only that type.

You might be wondering whether variables and parameters have to have different names. Within a particular procedure, they do. Parameter names are local to their procedure; as are local variables. They occupy the same *namespace*.

```
PROCEDURE Subtract(a, b: INTEGER; VAR difference: INTEGER);
        VAR a: INTEGER;
```

is illegal because the name 'a' is used as a parameter as well as for a local variable.

What about variables used as arguments? Can they have the same name as a procedure's parameters? Yes, they can. The original variables are out of the procedure's *scope*—the procedure can't "see" them; that is, the original variables are "hidden."

```
PROCEDURE Subtract(a, b: INTEGER;
                        VAR difference: INTEGER);
(* the parameter 'difference' is a local name; it is
only known within Subtract *)
BEGIN
...
END Subtract:

PROCEDURE Do*;
    VAR difference: INTEGER;
(* the variable 'difference' is local to Do *)
BEGIN
    Subtract(13, 3, difference) ;
...
END Do;
```

The identifier difference is used twice in the above program fragment. Each is local to its procedure—they are known only within that procedure—so there is no name conflict here. We will talk more about scope in the next chapter.

4.6   Value Parameters Versus Variable Parameters

The difference between value and variable parameters is an important concept.

A **value parameter** passes a *value* to a procedure. The value of the argument is *copied to the parameter*. It is the copy of the value that is used *locally* within the procedure; the original argument is not affected. Both literal values and variables can be used as arguments to value parameters. When a procedure *uses* a value, then the parameter should be declared as a value parameter.

A **variable parameter** passes a *reference* to the original value to a procedure. The value *is not copied*—the parameter becomes an *alias* to the original variable. Changes made to the parameter within the procedure affect the original value—whatever happens to the parameter also happens to the original variable. *Only variables may be passed as variable parameters.* When a procedure *changes* a value, then use a variable parameter.

For a variable parameter, it is normally a requirement that the types of the argument and the corresponding parameter must be *identical*. In the cases of records and pointers (which we haven't talked about yet), there are some exceptions to this rule, and we will talk about that in later chapters.

The reserved word VAR is used to indicate variable parameters. VAR has to appear only once on the list of parameters as long as the type doesn't change (i.e., encounter a semicolon). You need to have another VAR appear whenever there is a transition from one type to another.

```
PROCEDURE Proc (VAR x, y, z: CHAR; a, b, c: INTEGER);
(* x, y and z are variable parameters; but a, b and c
   are value parameters *)


PROCEDURE Proc2 (a: CHAR; VAR b: CHAR; c: CHAR);
(* a and c are value parameters while b is a variable
   parameter. Try to logically group parameters and
   give them meaningful names; Proc2 could be
   confusing to someone reading it. *)


PROCEDURE CopyInt(source: INTEGER;
                  VAR destination: INTEGER);
(* this is more clear as to what the purposes of the
   parameters are *)
```

Try grouping all value parameters together, as well as grouping all variable parameters together. This may help clarify the intentions of the parameters.

We said before that the value of variable parameters can be changed, but the value of value parameters can't be changed. This isn't entirely true. Actually, value parameters *can* be changed, but the change isn't "permanent." When an argument is passed as a value parameter, a *copy* of that value is assigned to the parameter. Let us look at an example:

```
MODULE OfeParmtest;

(* To demonstrate the differences between variable and value
   parameters *)

   IMPORT Out;

   PROCEDURE ChangeVal (valNumber: INTEGER);
   (* Attempt to change the value of a value parameter *)
   BEGIN
      valNumber := 10;
      Out.String("Inside ChangeVal number is ");
      Out.Int(number, 0); Out.Ln
   END ChangeVal;

   PROCEDURE ChangeVar (VAR varNumber: INTEGER);
   (* Changes the value of a variable parameter *)
   BEGIN
      varNumber := 20
   END ChangeVar;

   PROCEDURE Do*;
      VAR number: INTEGER;
   BEGIN
      number := 5;
      Out.String("Number is ");
      Out.Int(number, 0); Out.Ln;
      ChangeVal(number);
      Out.String("After ChangeVal number is ");
      Out.Int(number, 0); Out.Ln;
      ChangeVar(number);
      Out.String("After ChangeVar number is ");
      Out.Int(number, 0); Out.Ln;
   END Do;

END OfeParmtest.
```

Read through OfeParmtest and see if you can figure out what the output will be. Then compile it and run OfeParmtest.Do.

The output should look like this:

```
Number is 5
Inside ChangeVal valNumber is 10
After ChangeVal number is 5
After ChangeVar number is 20
```

In procedure Do, we first initialize number—it gets the value 5. Then we make a procedure call to ChangeVal.

During the call to ChangeVal, valNumber gets the value that number has. But valNumber and number are two completely separate entities. The value 5 is copied from number to valNumber, but their relationship ends there. If valNumber is changed inside of ChangeVal, the copy is changed, but not number; after ChangeVal ends, number is still 5.

Compare this to ChangeVar that uses a variable parameter. The call to ChangeVar *actually changes* the value of number. The two identifiers varNumber and number have a more intimate relationship—they refer to the exact same variable. While we are inside of ChangeVar, we call the variable varNumber —when inside of Do, we call the variable number; varNumber is an *alias* for number.

Can a variable parameter be used without it being changed? Yes. Nothing forces you to change variable parameters within the procedure. Generally, we want to avoid this because it can be confusing as to why it's declared as a VAR.

Sometimes, however, programmers will declare variable parameters that aren't changed for efficiency reasons. Remember that value parameters have to be copied, and often making a copy requires some "overhead." But in most cases, the rule is that value parameters are *used* and variable parameters are *changed*.

Can a value parameter be changed inside a procedure? Yes. But since value parameters are "copies," the changes aren't reflected in the original value. That is, changes are in effect only within the called procedure—when it returns the value has not been changed.

Parameter passing is an extremely important concept. So it is vital that you understand the difference between value and variable parameters. Let us look at another example:

There is a bug in the following module, try to find it.

```
MODULE OfeSwap;

(* Demonstrate swapping values using value parameters *)

  IMPORT Out;

  PROCEDURE Swap (first, second: INTEGER);
  (* swap the values of first and second *)
    VAR temp: INTEGER;
  BEGIN
    temp := first;
    first := second;
    second := temp
  END Swap;

  PROCEDURE Do*;
    VAR one, two: INTEGER;
  BEGIN
```

```
    one := 3; two := 7;
    Out.String("one is "); Out.Int(one, 0); Out.Ln;
    Out.String("two is "); Out.Int(two, 0); Out.Ln;
    Swap(one, two);
    Out.String("After Swap number is ");
    Out.String("one is "); Out.Int(one, 0); Out.Ln;
    Out.String("two is "); Out.Int(two, 0); Out.Ln
END Do;
```

```
END OfeSwap.
```

If you can't find the bug, try compiling and running OfeSwap.Do.

What is supposed to happen during procedure Do? It is supposed to take the values of two numbers—one and two—and swap them. At the end of the program, one *should* be 7 and two *should* be 3. But that's not what happens. Why not?

The problem is that Swap is declared with *value parameters*. Any changes we make inside of Swap are only temporary—we're swapping the values of the copies first and second; one and two are left unchanged. To fix Swap you need to declare it as

```
    PROCEDURE Swap (VAR first, second: INTEGER);
```

so that both first and second are variable parameters. Then after the call Swap(one, two), one and two are changed.

Question: Why do we need the variable temp in Swap? What purpose does it serve?

Answer: You can't just swap first with second. One of the values would be lost. For instance, if you just assigned one value to the other,

```
    first := second;
    second := first;
```

what would happen? In the first assignment, first gets the value of second. At that point, both first and second have the same value! The original value of first is gone. Then in the second assignment, first is assigned to second which really doesn't accomplish anything—they had the same value already. We need temp to temporarily hold the value of first so that we don't lose it.

4.7   Exercises

1. In your own words, describe what a variable is and why it is useful.

2. Describe the similarities and differences between changing a value via a procedure call and changing a value via an assignment statement.

3. Describe the differences between variable parameters and value parameters.

4. Write procedures Subtract and Multiply in a manner similar to OfeAdder.Add.

5. Write a procedure that converts stellar distances measured in light years to miles. You may use 186,000 miles per second as the constant for the speed of light.

6. Write a procedure that converts seconds to hours and a procedure that converts from minutes to seconds.

7. Write procedures that convert from Fahrenheit temperature to Celsius and vice versa. Formulas are: $F = 9/5*C + 32$ and $C = 5/9*(F - 32)$.

8. Write a procedure that converts a fractional value to a decimal one. (*Hint*: Pass the numerator and denominator as separate arguments.)

9. Write modules to test the procedures from exercises 4-8.

Chapter 5
Using Modules

5.1   Module In

Module In comes with most Oberon compilers, just like module Out. However, module In can be just a little bit trickier to work with than module Out.

Input and output used to be simpler before the invention of multiwindowed user interfaces. Module Out isn't too bad—we can always write to the same place. But input can be more complicated: Where should the input come from? Which window is the input window? How do we collect what the user types in?

The answers to these questions can be found in the documentation that comes with your compiler. On my system, module In takes its input from a *highlighted selection,* or, if there isn't a selection, then input comes from the text window that is currently "in focus."

Modules In and Out are supplied with most Oberon compilers to simplify learning the Oberon language. They are meant to be learning tools, and so most compilers have additional module libraries that do more sophisticated input and output. Once you are comfortable with the Oberon language, you can start learning those modules. In the meantime, Out and In are sufficient for our needs.

The definition of In is,

```
DEFINITION In;

  VAR Done: BOOLEAN;

  PROCEDURE Open;
  PROCEDURE Char (VAR ch: CHAR);
  PROCEDURE Int (VAR i: INTEGER);
  PROCEDURE LongInt (VAR l: LONGINT);
  PROCEDURE Real (VAR x: REAL);
  PROCEDURE Name (VAR name: ARRAY OF CHAR);
  PROCEDURE String (VAR str: ARRAY OF CHAR);

END In.
```

Let us look at this module in detail. First of all, what do you think this statement means?

```
VAR Done: BOOLEAN;
```

It is a variable definition—only it's not inside any procedure. Done is what is known as a **global variable**—it can be used anywhere within module In. And because Done has been exported (we know it has been exported because it appears in the definition of In), any other module that imports In can also access Done.

When referring to Done from within module In, we need use only the name Done, but from other modules, we have to use In.Done. The global variable must be qualified with the module name, just like procedures.

To export global variables, simply follow the variable name with the export mark '*'; for example,

```
VAR Done*: BOOLEAN;
    errorType*: INTEGER;
```

In.Done is used to express the state of the input process. We can look at it to see if what we attempted to do actually worked. That is, this variable indicates whether the most recent input operation has succeeded. It is set to TRUE by a successful call to In.Open, and set to FALSE by the first unsuccessful input operation. Once set to FALSE, it stays that way until the next call to In.Open. This is how we can check whether we have actually read in a value.

The procedures are, for the most part, analogous to the procedures from module Out. There are procedures to read in most of the basic types. Notice that all of the procedures have variable parameters.

Procedures In.Name and In.String do slightly different things. In.String reads in a string, but stops when it encounters **whitespace**—a space, tab, or newline character. If the string being read is enclosed in quotes, however, the entire string is read in. In.Name is similar to In.String, only it fails if the string read in isn't a valid Oberon identifier name.

The following is an example using In:

```
MODULE OfeIn;

(* Demonstrate the use of module In *)

  IMPORT In, Out;

  PROCEDURE Do*;
  (* Read in a bunch of different kinds of values, and then
     write them to the log *)
  VAR int: INTEGER; ch: CHAR; rl: REAL;
      string: ARRAY 20 OF CHAR;
  BEGIN
    In.Open;
```

```
            In.Int(int);
            In.Char(ch);
            In.Real(rl);
            In.String(string);
            Out.Int(int, 0); Out.Ln;
            Out.Char(ch); Out.Ln;
            Out.Real(rl, 0); Out.Ln;
            Out.String(string); Out.Ln
        END Do;

END OfeIn.
```

Compile the above module, and use

```
100R 3.14 "hello world"
```

as input. Typically, you will have to first highlight the above text, and then execute the command OfeIn.Do. But first check your system's documentation.

Most of OfeIn should be relatively easy to follow. Within procedure Do, In.Open is invoked to open the input "source." Then four different procedures are used to read in values for variables `int`, `ch`, `rl`, and `string`. Those values are then written back out to the log.

One thing I should point out about In.String (and a few of the other procedures we have talked about); it has a parameter of type ARRAY OF CHAR—why don't we need to specify a length? For arrays used as parameters, *the length is determined by the length of the argument passed during the procedure call.* That way we aren't limited to passing arrays of the same size all the time. Character arrays of any size can be used as a parameter to In.String.

5.2   Modules and Program Structure

Modules can be thought of as a package of data (variables) and operations (procedures) that is meant to be imported and used by other modules.

But a module is more than just a collection of declarations. Modules help us to organize our programs and break them up into pieces we can deal with more easily. Modules provide structure to our programs and mechanisms to support the concepts of *data abstraction* and *information hiding*. We have already touched on these ideas briefly—although we haven't really defined what they are as of yet. We will continue to expand on these ideas as we progress through this book.

Modules have another benefit by providing a unit for **separate compilation**. Modules can be compiled one at a time; they don't need to be compiled all at once. This means you have to compile only modules that have been changed, which is a great benefit as your "programs" get larger and larger.

Because the module is such an important concept in Oberon, let us look at it more detail.

Modules and procedures are actually very similar in structure. For instance, variables can be defined on the module level (as we have seen in module In) and are called **global variables**. They are defined in exactly the same way as local variables are defined within procedures. The reserved word VAR is followed by the variable definitions.

```
VAR status: BOOLEAN; counter: INTEGER;
    description: ARRAY 80 OF CHAR;
```

It is usually a good idea to try to limit the use of global variables as much as possible. Programs can get very confusing when trying to juggle a large number of global variables. When they are necessary, then the variable definitions should appear before all the procedure declarations.

The module's IMPORT statement must come before any variable definitions or procedure declarations. So the basic format a module should have is

```
MODULE <module name>;

  IMPORT <import list>;

  VAR <global variable list>;

  <procedure declarations>

BEGIN

...

END <module name>.
```

Did you notice the use of the reserved word BEGIN? Modules can have *bodies*—just like procedures. After all of the variable definitions and procedure declarations, a single BEGIN can appear. This starts a block of statements that are executed as soon as the module is loaded into memory, that is, as soon as any of the module's procedures are called or global variables are used.

What is a module body used for? Since most actions in Oberon are initiated by commands, a module's body is usually used only to initialize global variables. Remember, we want to initialize *all* variables before they are used, and global variables are no exception. The module body is the best place to perform this initialization.

Modules and procedures are very similar, but there are differences. Procedures can't have IMPORT statements (any importing affects the entire module), procedures must appear inside a module (modules are at the "outermost level"), and because declarations within a procedure are local to that procedure, export marks are meaningless—and are ignored by the compiler.

Modules cannot appear inside other modules. That is, modules cannot be *nested*. However, procedures *can* appear inside other procedures. When a procedure is declared within another procedure, it is known as a **local procedure**. Just like local variables, local procedures are visible only within the procedure where it is declared.

Most of the time, there is little reason to declare local procedures—so we won't give any examples here.

5.3   The Import List and Qualified Identifiers

All imported procedures and variables must be qualified by the exporting module's name, so it can get tedious when those module names are very long. Therefore, there is an alternate form of naming, called *aliasing*, that can be used in the import list,

```
IMPORT <alias> := <module name>;
```

In this form, the imported module is known under the alias within the importing module.

```
IMPORT O := Out, M := Math; D := Display;

PROCEDURE Show*;
    VAR a, b: REAL;
BEGIN
    a := M.Sqrt(b);      (* equivalent to Math.Sqrt(b) *)
    D.Open;              (* equivalent to Display.Open *)
    O.Real(a); O.Ln     (* equivalent to Out.Real(a); Out.Ln
                            *)
END Show;
```

You still need to qualify the imported identifiers, but aliases can help keep names to a more manageable length.

The advantages of qualified names are always knowing which module an object is imported from, and keeping objects that have the same name from conflicting with each other. These advantages are worth the effort of qualifying all of our imported objects with the module name.

Recall that in Oberon, the qualified identifier `ModuleName.VarName` is different from the *simple identifier* `VarName`. So, we can define `VarName` in as many modules as we want, with as many meanings as we need; there is no problem with naming conflicts as long as each identifier is declared *once and only once* within a particular module.

```
In.String(name);
Out.String(name);
```

It is possible to have a `String` procedure defined in both In and Out because, by qualifying each procedure call with the module name, we know exactly which procedure we mean in all cases. We could have a `String` procedure in every module we write if we wanted, and always know exactly which String procedure we mean—the qualifying module name uniquely identifies which procedure to call.

5.4   Forward Declarations

Oberon compilers can be implemented as what are called **one-pass compilers**—the source text is processed *once* from beginning to end; the compiler can't "look ahead" to see what's declared later on. In modules written for one-pass compilers, a procedure or variable needs to be declared before it can be used. This works out very well in most cases, but occasionally we may want to use a procedure *before* the actual procedure declaration.

We can do this in Oberon by providing a **forward declaration**—the procedure itself is declared, but the procedure's body is not written until later in the source text. To specify that we mean a forward declaration, we use the symbol '^' (on some Oberon systems, the character '^' appears as an upward pointing arrow '↑').

```
PROCEDURE^ Forward(<parameter list>);
```

Later on, when the actual declaration occurs—when the body of the procedure is specified—the procedure heading must have *exactly* the same name and formal parameter list. Note that forward declarations are not *required* by the Oberon language; their use is dependent on the implementation. They may or may not be required by your compiler.

```
(* three forward declarations *)
PROCEDURE^ One(first: CHAR);
PROCEDURE^ Two(first, second: INTEGER);
PROCEDURE^ None;
...

(* and the corresponding actual declarations *)
PROCEDURE One(first: CHAR);
BEGIN
...
END One;

PROCEDURE Two(first, second: INTEGER);
BEGIN
...
END Two;


PROCEDURE None;
```

```
BEGIN
  . . .
END None;
```

5.5   Writing Modules

When writing modules (and procedures), there are some things that should be kept in mind:

- They should be easy to check and test.
- They should be able to be read and understood—not only by the person writing the module, but by other programmers as well.
- They should work as intended.
- They should have appropriate comments (but don't always believe what the comments tell you).

Don't be afraid to experiment with programming. Take some of the example modules and try modifying them. Most people believe that you can't learn to program without actually writing programs. It's like learning to drive a car—you need to get behind the wheel.

Modules should be written to be readable and in a clear style. Good formatting and meaningful identifier names go a long way in helping to meet these goals. Consistent use of indenting and appropriate use of comments to explain the less obvious parts are also important. Proper use of procedures can significantly reduce program complexity.

Read other people's modules and the examples that come with your compiler. It is a great help in learning what to do as well as what not to do.

5.6   Exercises

1.   Examine the procedures in modules In and Out that take an ARRAY OF CHAR as an argument. Explain why there is no array length specified and why it might be a bad idea to require such a length.

2.   Write a procedure that uses module In to read in a row of up to 10 characters and then write them back out in reverse order.

3.   Write a procedure that uses module In to read in five numbers, adds them together, and then writes out the total.

4.   Explain the benefits of separate compilations of modules.

5. Describe the differences between modules and procedures. In what ways are they similar?

6. Explain the uses and advantages of global variables. Then do the same for local variables.

7. Why do you think the IMPORT statement comes before variable definitions and procedure declarations?

8. Can you think of any other uses for a module's body (its BEGIN-END block), other than for global variable initialization?

9. Write a module to test out the procedures you wrote in exercises 2 and 3. Use aliasing in the import list so that you can write I.Char, O.Char, etc., rather than the full module names.

10. Describe qualified identifiers and explain their advantages and disadvantages.

11. Test whether your compiler requires forward declarations by writing a module in which a procedure is called before it is declared. If your compiler requires a forward declaration, write one so that your module works properly without reordering the way the procedures are declared.

Chapter 6
Expressions and Function Procedures

6.1   Expressions

Expressions represent or show a value; like everything in Oberon, all expressions have a type. The simplest expressions are literal values. Variables are also expressions.

There is a class of procedures that can be used as expressions; these are called *function procedures*. Let us take a look at an example using a function procedure.

```
MODULE OfeFunction;

(* Demonstrate function procedures *)

    IMPORT Out;

    PROCEDURE Squared(x: REAL): REAL;
    (* Squares a number *)
    BEGIN
       RETURN x * x
    END Squared;

    PROCEDURE Do*;
    (* Calls Squared and displays the result *)
       VAR real: REAL;
    BEGIN
       real := Squared(4);
       Out.Real(real, 0);
       Out.String(" is 4 squared."); Out.Ln
    END Do;

END OfeFunction.
```

Once again, read over OfeFunction and try to figure out what it does. Then compile it and run OfeFunction.Do.

The following (or something similar) should be written in the log,

```
1.6E+01 is 4 squared.
```

In OfeFunction, we have declared the function procedure Squared(). There are two things that make it different from the procedures we have declared before.

First, in the procedure declaration, there is an additional type name following the closing parenthesis. This is the *result type* of the procedure. It is the presence of a result type that makes Squared() a function procedure. It specifies what type of value the procedure will return.

Second, within the body of the procedure is the reserved word RETURN followed by an expression. The RETURN statement sets the actual value that the function procedure is to return. In this case, we want to return the square of the argument, so we multiply x by itself.

If there had been other statements following RETURN in Squared(), they would not have been executed. The RETURN statement actually does two things, it sets the value of the result, and also ends the procedure's execution. RETURN forces the function procedure to "return" to the point from which it was called.

Within procedure Do, the call to Squared() returns a result that is assigned to `real`. The result value of any function procedure call can be treated like any other expression— as a value with a particular type.

6.2   Operators and Precedence

As we have seen previously, arithmetic operators can be used to form expressions. Let us review these operators and examine them in more detail.

The operators for real numbers (types REAL and LONGREAL) are +, −, *, and /.

The operators for integer numbers (types SHORTINT, INTEGER, and LONGINT) are +, −, *, DIV, and MOD.

But a minus sign can also be used to express negative numbers or to negate terms for both real and integer values,

```
-1            (* negative 1 *)
-3.14         (* negative 3.14 *)
-(5 + 6)      (* evaluates to negative 11 *)
```

DIV gives the *quotient* of integer division.

MOD gives the *remainder* of integer division.

Integer division on positive numbers is straightforward. But when dealing with negative numbers, it can get tricky. In fact, because mathematics does not provide a definition for integer division by negative numbers, neither does Oberon. This means that, for example,

```
a := 5 DIV 3; b := 5 MOD 3;   (* OK. a = 1 and b = 2 *)
a := -5 DIV 3; b := -5 MOD 3; (* OK. a = -2 and b = 1 *)
```

But,

```
a := 5 DIV -3; b := 5 MOD -3;    (* ? a = ? and b = ? *)
a := -5 DIV -3; b := -5 MOD -3; (* ? a = ? and b = ? *)
```

are technically illegal—although you probably won't get either compile-time or run-time errors. a and b will be set to some value, but you can't be sure what your system will set them to. These values are implementation dependent.

Of course, integer division by zero is illegal and will result in an error.

Operands for all of the arithmetic operators can be *constants*, variables, or *function procedures*; that is, any expression that can be evaluated to a value of the proper type.

Operands in arithmetic expressions must have compatible types *and* must be the correct type for the operators employed. Operations are performed in a (generally) left-to-right fashion based on operator **precedence**—the order in which operators are evaluated. It is just like you might remember from basic math, multiplication and division are worked out before addition and subtraction.

Oberon has four *levels* of precedence. The operator '~' has the highest precedence, followed by the multiplicative operators (*, /, DIV, MOD, and also as we shall see later the & operator), then additive operators (+, −, and also the OR operator), and finally *relational operators*. We haven't talked about ~, &, OR, or relational operators yet, but we will get to them very soon. Operators of the same precedence are evaluated from left to right.

A table will help to show the precedence levels. The higher up in the table, the higher the precedence of the operator.

Table 6.1: Operator Precedence

Operators	Classification
~	negation
*, /, DIV, MOD, &	multiplicative
+, −, OR	additive
=, #, <, <=, >, >=, IN, IS	relational

Don't worry that you don't recognize all of the operators yet. To illustrate the effects of precedence, let us look at some examples.

```
    3 - 5 * 4
⇨   3 - (5 * 4)
⇨   3 - 20
⇨   -17
```

Multiplication has higher precedence, so it is done first.

```
    2 * 3 + 12 DIV 3
```

```
⇨  (2 * 3) + (12 DIV 3)
⇨  6 + 4
⇨  10
```

From left to right, multiplication and division are done first, and then addition.

```
   66 - 11 * 3 + 15 / 5
⇨  66 - (11 * 3) + (15 / 5)
⇨  66 - 33 + 3.0
⇨  36.0
```

Do you know why the answer to the last example is 36.0 instead of 36? Notice that we used real division ('/') rather than integer division ('DIV'). Real division produces a real number as a result even if both operands are integers.

Parentheses may be used to change the order of evaluation. That is, you can override the precedence rules by using parentheses.

```
   6 + (8 - 7)
⇨  6 + 1
⇨  7

   8 * ((9 DIV 3) + 4)
⇨  8 * (3 + 4)
⇨  8 * 7
⇨  56

   8 * ((9 MOD 3) + 4)
⇨  8 * (0 + 4)
⇨  8 * 4
⇨  32
```

Because of precedence rules, when the minus sign is used to express negative numbers you usually have to use parentheses. Recall that the minus sign has lower precedence than multiplication and division, and has the same precedence as the plus sign.

```
3 + -4        (* ERROR!! Compiler expects a number
               after the '+', not another operator *)

3 + (-4)      (* OK. Parentheses force the '-4' to be
               evaluated before doing the addition *)

3 + 4         (* OK. The compiler evaluates additive
               operators from left to right *)

(-3) + 4      (* OK. Parentheses make the evaluation
               order explicit *)
```

```
-3 * 4                    (* OK. But remember that the compiler
                          sees this as '-(3 * 4)' not '(-3) * 4'
                          because '*' has higher precedence than
                          '-' *)
```

It is usually a good idea to use parentheses to help clarify complicated expressions—even when they may not be required.

```
7 + 8 - 3 * 9 MOD 4 DIV 3 + 5 * 2 - 1
```

What is the intention of the above expression? It is difficult to read.

```
7 + 8 - (((3 * 9) MOD 4) DIV 3) + (5 * 2) - 1
```

This second expression evaluates in exactly the same manner as the first, but is somewhat easier to read. The actual evaluation is presented here,

```
⇨  7 + 8 - ((27 MOD 4) DIV 3) + 10 - 1
⇨  7 + 8 - (3 DIV 3) + 10 - 1
⇨  7 + 8 - 1 + 10 - 1
⇨  23
```

6.3   Function Procedures

Function procedures—or simply *functions*—are very much like the proper procedures we have talked about. Functions can be predeclared, provided by library modules, or can be written by any programmer.

The difference between proper procedures and function procedures is that **function procedures** *return a result*. A call to a function procedure, complete with its arguments, represents a value that is returned to the point from which the function was called. This makes a function procedure a kind of expression—its value can be assigned to a variable or used as an argument in another procedure call.

A function declaration must *always* have parentheses, even if it has no parameters. Similarly, a function call must always have parentheses, even if it has no arguments.

Function procedures must always be declared with a single result type—multiple values cannot be returned. The result type of a function procedure must be a simple type— one of the basic types or a pointer type—arrays and records cannot be the result of function procedures. Pointers, arrays, and records are discussed in later chapters.

Note: The types of the parameters are *completely separate* from the type of result. They are independent decisions that can be made in a function declaration.

Here are some examples of valid declarations:

```
IsEven(int: INTEGER): BOOLEAN;
StringLength(string: ARRAY OF CHAR): LONGINT;
```

```
SquareRoot(rl: REAL): LONGREAL;
Round(number: REAL; places: INTEGER): REAL;
```

The RETURN statement is used to specify the value that the function returns,

```
RETURN <expression>;
```

where <expression> is any expression that evaluates to a type compatible with the result type of the function. Function procedures must have at least one return statement, which expresses explicitly the value that is to be returned.

```
RETURN TRUE;        (* return a boolean value *)
RETURN 1;           (* return the number '1' *)
RETURN x;           (* return the value of the
                       variable x *)
RETURN  x  *  (y + z); (* return the value of the
evaluated expression *)
```

Note, however, that RETURN can appear in proper procedures as well. In the case of proper procedures, <expression> is an empty statement. That is,

```
RETURN;
```

The return statement ends the procedure and control returns to the point where the procedure was called.

Many times, a single result isn't enough—we may need two or more values calculated from a procedure call. Because functions can return only a single result, it is a temptation to also change the values of the arguments via variable parameters. However, as a matter of convention, function procedures shouldn't have variable parameters—that is, they should not have *side-effects*. Otherwise, it can be confusing as to what is the purpose of the function. If you need to return multiple values, it is better to use proper procedures with several variable parameters.

A word of caution: Procedures shouldn't inadvertently call themselves. This could put the program into an **infinite loop**—the program would continue to execute indefinitely. When a procedure calls itself, this is known as **recursion**. Making a *recursive call* when you don't intend to is dangerous; yet there are times when we may want to use recursion. We shall discuss uses for recursion in a later chapter.

6.4   Other Standard Procedures

The following table lists the *predeclared procedures*. Some are **generic procedures**, which apply to several types of operands. v stands for a variable, x and n for expressions, and T for a type.

Table 6.2: Function procedures

Name	Argument type	Result type	Function
ABS(x)	numeric type	type of x	absolute value
ASH(x, n)	x, n: integer type	LONGINT	arithmetic shift $(x * 2^n)$
CAP(x)	CHAR	CHAR	x is letter: corresponding capital letter
CHR(x)	integer type	CHAR	character with ordinal number x
ENTIER(x)	real type	LONGINT	largest integer not greater than x
LEN(v, n)	v: array;	LONGINT	length of v in dimension n. n: integer, constant (first dimension = 0)
LEN(v)	v: array	LONGINT	equivalent to LEN(v, 0)
LONG(x)	SHORTINT INTEGER REAL	INTEGER LONGINT LONGREAL	identity
MAX(T)	T = basic type T = SET	T INTEGER	maximum value of type T, or maximum element of a set
MIN(T)	T = basic type T = SET	T INTEGER	minimum value of type T, or 0
ODD(x)	integer type	BOOLEAN	x MOD 2 = 1
ORD(x)	CHAR	INTEGER	ordinal number of x
SHORT(x)	LONGINT INTEGER LONGREAL	INTEGER SHORTINT REAL	identity (truncation possible)
SIZE(T)	any type	integer type	number of bytes required by T

Table 6.3: Proper procedures

Name	Argument types	Function
ASSERT(x)	x: Boolean expression	terminate program execution if not x
ASSERT(x, n)	x: Boolean expression; n: integer constant	terminate program execution if not x
COPY(x, v)	x: character array, string; v: character array	v := x
DEC(v)	integer type	v := v - 1
DEC(v, n)	v, n: integer type	v := v - n
EXCL(v, x)	v: SET; x: integer type	v := v - {x}
HALT(n)	integer constant	terminate program execution
INC(v)	integer type	v := v + 1
INC(v, n)	v, n: integer type	v := v + n
INCL(v, x)	v: SET; x: integer type	v := v + {x}
NEW(v)	pointer to record or fixed array	allocate v ^
NEW(v, x_0, ..., x_n)	v: pointer to open array; x_i: integer type	allocate v ^ with lengths x_0 ... x_n

Let us look more closely at the function procedures.

ABS(x) returns the absolute value of v, this is a common mathematical function. Assuming i, j, k: INTEGER,

```
i := 3; j := 4;
k := ABS(i + j);        (* k is 7 *)
i := ABS(-7);           (* i is 7 *)
```

ASH() is arithmetic shift. It is used to manipulate values on the bit level. We won't go into details on its usage because it is "low-level."

CAP(x) is used to convert character values from lower-case letters to upper-case letters. If a character is a lower-case letter, CAP(x) returns the equivalent upper-case letter. Otherwise, if it is an upper-case letter, it returns the original value. Be careful of characters that aren't letters; they may be "converted" even though they aren't letters. Assuming a, b, c: CHAR,

```
a := "a"; b := "B";
c := CAP(a);        (* c is "A" *)
c := CAP(b);        (* c is "B" *)
c := CAP("&");      (* c is 06X (at least using the two
                       compilers I tested this on)  *)
```

CHR(x) returns the character at ordinal position x; which is similar to using hex values for characters. Only in this case, x is a decimal value rather than a hex value. Assuming ch: CHAR,

```
ch := CHR(65);    (* ch is "A" which is 41X in ASCII *)
```

ENTIER() is used for converting real types to integer types. Most of the time, this means some information—the part after the decimal point—is lost. This is similar to rounding, except you always round *down*. The more formal way to say it is ENTIER(x) returns the largest integer not greater than x. Assuming i: INTEGER,

```
i := ENTIER( 3.14 );     (* i is 3 *)
i := ENTIER( 5.0 );      (* i is 5 *)
i := ENTIER( -7.35 );    (* i is -8 *)
```

LEN() will be examined more closely in the chapter on arrays. LEN(v) returns the *total* number of elements in—or the length of—array v. For character arrays, this isn't the same thing as the length of the string. The length of the string is determined by the position of the terminating character 0X, which is *at most* LEN(v) − 1. Remember that we have to always leave space for the 0X. Assuming v: ARRAY 32 OF CHAR and i: LONGINT,

```
i := LEN(v);     (* i is 32 *)
v := "Not 32";   (* string length is 6 *)
i := LEN(v);     (* but array length is still 32 *)
```

LONG() is used to convert smaller numeric types to larger numeric types: SHORTINT to INTEGER, INTEGER to LONGINT, or REAL to LONGREAL. LONG() conversions are handled automatically in most cases. Assuming i, j: INTEGER and lInt: LONGINT,

```
lInt := LONG(i) * LONG(j);
(* explicitly converting values of i and j to
LONGINT before multiplying *)
```

MAX() and MIN() are used to access the maximum and minimum values for basic types; that is, to determine their limits. These are necessary because maximum and minimum values are implementation dependent. Assuming i: INTEGER,

```
i := MAX(INTEGER);
(*  i  is  32768  on  my  system,  it  could  be
different on yours *)

i := MIN(INTEGER);
(* i is -32767 on my system *)
```

ODD(x) returns TRUE if x is an odd number, and FALSE if it is even. Assuming b: BOOLEAN,

```
b := ODD(3);                (* b is TRUE *)
```

ORD(x) does exactly the opposite of CHR(x); ORD(x) returns the ordinal position of character x. Assuming i: INTEGER,

```
i := ORD("A");    (* i is 65 for ASCII characters *)
```

SHORT() is used when attempting to convert from a larger numeric type to a smaller type—just the opposite of LONG(). So a LONGREAL could be converted to a REAL, LONGINT to INTEGER, or INTEGER to SHORTINT. Information could potentially be lost in this conversion—values could be truncated.

```
i := SHORT(lInt);
(* necessary to assign LONGINT to INTEGER *)
```

SIZE(T) returns how many bytes are required by the system to store a value of type T. Just like MAX() and MIN(), this information is implementation dependent. This information is sometimes required for *low-level programming*. Assuming i: INTEGER,

```
i := SIZE(REAL);   (* i is 4 on my system *)
```

Now let us look at the proper procedures.

ASSERT(x, n) is used to end a program based on the evaluation of some condition x. We will look more at ASSERT later on.

COPY allows the assignment of a string or a character array containing a terminating 0X to another character array. In COPY(x, v), x is the *source* and v is the *destination*. That is, x is copied to v. COPY stops when it encounters the terminating 0X character, or when it reaches the end of either x or v. If necessary, the assigned value of x is truncated to the length of v − 1. The destination v will always have 0X as a terminator. Assuming s1, s2: ARRAY 9 OF CHAR,

```
COPY("Oberon", s1);       (* s1 is "Oberon" *)
```

```
COPY("Eric Nikitin", s2);
(*  s2  is  "Eric  Nik".  s2  isn't  long  enough  for
the rest *)


COPY(s1, s2);              (* s2 is "Oberon *)
```

DEC is used to decrement integer variables. That is, decrease or make it smaller by a fixed amount. DEC(v) is equivalent to v := v − 1, and we could actually do it that way instead. But because increasing and decreasing *counters* is a very common programming task, we have a special procedure to do it for us. DEC(v, n) decreases v by n instead of 1. That is, DEC(v, n) is equivalent to v := v − n. Assuming i: INTEGER,

```
i := 20;
DEC(i);              (* i is 19 *)
DEC(i, 5);           (* i is 14 *)
DEC(i, 2);           (* i is 12 *)
DEC(i, 1);           (* i is 11. This is the same as
                     if we'd used DEC(i) *)
```

EXCL and INCL are used for set types—which we haven't talked about. So, we will save these for later.

HALT(n) is similar to ASSERT. However, HALT ends the program *unconditionally*. That is, it always ends the program when it is encountered in a statement sequence. The meaning of the number n in both ASSERT and HALT is implementation dependent.

INC is the opposite of DEC. INC is used to increment integer variables—make them bigger by a fixed amount. INC(v) is equivalent to v := v + 1, and INC(v, n) is equivalent to v := v + n.

```
i := 0;
INC(i);              (* i is 1 *)
INC(i, 4);           (* i is 5 *)
INC(i, 1);           (* i is 6, the same as if we'd
                     used INC(i) *)
```

NEW is beyond what we know at this point. We will discuss NEW in chapter 15.

6.5   Constant Expressions

The definition of *constant expressions* is similar to the definition of variables. A **constant expression** represents a value, and is associated with an identifier. The constant's value *cannot be changed* during program execution. Therefore, the constant must have a value that can be determined at compile time.

Constant definitions begin with the reserved word CONST followed by an identifier, an equals sign, and then the value in the form of an expression. A semicolon separates successive definitions. Constants are treated as having an appropriate type for the value they represent.

```
CONST
    pi = 3.14;                            (* REAL constant *)
    stringLength = 20;                    (* INTEGER constant *)
    maxLength = stringLength - 1;         (* INTEGER constant *)
    interestRate = 0.0725;                (* REAL constant *)
    tab = 09X;                            (* CHAR constant *)
    authorName = "Eric Nikitin";          (* string constant *)
```

After the constants have been defined, they may be used throughout the module wherever that type of value is permitted. Constants can be used almost exactly like variables, except that their value can never be changed. They can't be assigned to or used as an argument to a variable parameter. But they *can* be used any place a literal value of compatible type is expected.

```
    VAR string: ARRAY stringLength OF CHAR;
    . . .
    circumference = 2 * pi * radius;
    simpleInterest = principal * interestRate;
    Out.String(authorName);
```

Expressions can be used in constant definitions as long as the value can be determined at compile time. So, predeclared procedures and arithmetic operators can be used as long as operands are constant or literal values,

```
CONST
    maxSize = 10000;
    doubleSize = 2 * maxSize;
    (* doubleSize has value 20000 *)
    negSize = -maxSize; (* negSize has value -10000 *)
    divSize  = maxSize / 5; (* divSize has value 2000 *)
    nextDivSize = divSize + 1; (* nextDivSize = 2001 *)
```

Constants are helpful for several reasons. They can make values more meaningful—interestRate may be more clear than 0.0725. This makes programs "self-documenting"—clearer and easier to understand.

Constants also help with program maintenance, if the value you wished to use for pi changed to 3.141592, for example, then you would have to change it in only one place.

Also, just like variables, constants can be exported. Perhaps a math library module would contain the value of pi so that it needs to be defined in only one place. Simply follow the constant's name by the export mark '*',

```
CONST
    pi* = 3.141592;
```

When exported constant names are used in other modules, they need to be prefixed with the module name, just like any other qualified identifier,

```
circumference = 2 * Math.pi * radius;
```

Note that constants may be declared *local to a procedure*, just like a local variable. This is not a common practice, but is permitted in Oberon.

6.6   Scope

The realm of meaning of an identifier is known as its **scope**, where declared identifiers are visible and can be accessed. This includes constant, variable, and procedure names. The scope of an identifier is the portion of a program—called a **block**—where it is recognized. A module is a block, and procedures form blocks within a module.

When a procedure is declared, it forms a new block within a module. The procedure's name is outside the new block, and its parameters, local variables and statements are inside. However, recall that a *local procedure* can be defined within another procedure—and would thus be known only within the enclosing procedure. A local procedure then forms its own block completely enclosing its parameters, local variables, and statements.

An identifier can be declared only *once* within a block. If a particular identifier is declared in an enclosing block as well, it is hidden and cannot be accessed within the inner block.

```
MODULE OfeBlock;

   VAR x, y: INTEGER;

   PROCEDURE Outer;
      VAR x, z: REAL;
      PROCEDURE Inner;
         VAR x, w: CHAR;
      BEGIN
         . . .
      END Inner;
   BEGIN
      . . .
   END Outer;

END OfeBlock.
```

Examine OfeBlock. The variable x is defined in three different scopes—at the module level, in procedure Outer, and in procedure Inner. At any of these levels, only *one* version of x is ever visible at any one time. When within procedure Inner, only the x that is defined locally is visible. The integer variable x (from the module level) and real variable x (from the 'Outer' level) *cannot be reached at all*. They are completely hidden at that point.

However, y is defined in the *global block* (at the module level) and is visible not only within Outer, but within Inner as well. There are no other versions of y anyplace, so it is never hidden. However, it would be hidden in an inner block if the identifier y were declared at the local level.

The variable z is visible not only within Outer, but within Inner as well. Because z and Inner are declared locally in the same block, z can be used by Inner. However, z is invisible—and in fact does not even exist—relative to the module scope.

The variable w is usable only by Inner. It is locally defined and cannot be used anywhere else.

Understanding scope can be a little confusing, which is one of the reasons why you should avoid declaring local procedures. Scoping can be easier to understand if you try to limit declarations to two basic levels—the module level and the procedure level.

Modules from the import list are always imported in the global block—the import statement can appear only at the module level. Therefore, imported modules and their qualified identifiers are recognized within the entire importing module.

6.7   Program Planning

A good deal of programming involves planning how programs (modules and procedures) will be put together.

Well-designed software doesn't just happen—you have to plan ahead. We write software to solve a problem. This means structuring and designing a solution to that problem *before* actually starting to write the source text.

There are many commonly used techniques for helping with this structuring and design. Abstraction is one such method of organizing a program and dealing with complex problems.

Abstraction is viewing a problem and its solution as a set of *essential characteristics*. You don't have to view the entire problem all at once—you can break the problem into smaller pieces that are more easily understood. We can concentrate on what gets done instead of how it gets done (separate interface from implementation, as we have mentioned before). We can use procedures to act on data, rather than try to juggle complex data structures ourselves.

A benefit of abstraction is that we can often solve a problem once and then reuse that solution over and over again in similar circumstances. We can create module libraries that contain whole or partial solutions to our common problems.

We will discuss more on the concept of abstraction as we progress through this book.

One more note, when writing the solutions to problems, we want to provide understandable and *readable* source text. After all, the source text is the expression of the final solution to the problem. To improve program clarity, try to use meaningful identifier names, and format your modules so they are easy to read.

This means you should make the most of whitespace and indentation—neither of these matter to the compiler, but make a lot of difference to human readers. All whitespace is treated the same by the compiler—a space is as good as a tab. You should attempt to write modules in a readable format, as is done in this book. This is especially important as your modules get longer and more complicated.

6.8   Exercises

1. Explain the difference between function procedures and proper procedures.

2. Evaluate the following expressions using Oberon's precedence rules and state the type of the result.

```
a. 4 + 7 * 9 / 3 - 8 / 2 + 9 - 8 * 2 / 8
b. 20 * 7 + 9 * 6 - 10 + 9 * 9 - 7 * 7
c. 45 MOD 5 + 9 - 92 DIV 7 - 86 MOD 2 + 4
d. -13 + 20 - 55 + 8 / 5 - 3 * 8 + 34
e. -7 + 9 - 50 DIV + 7 MOD 5 + 12
f. -10 * 2 + 69 MOD 19 DIV 3 * 54
g. 29 * 70 / 2 * 33 / 8
h. 72 DIV 16 MOD 3 * 10 MOD 7 * 23 MOD 2
```

3. Write a function that, when given a positive real number, will return the "closest" integer value. That is, write a "rounding" function which will round down when the decimal part is less than 0.5 and round up otherwise. For example,

```
        Round( 3.14 )      results in 3
        Round( 3.54 )      results in 4
```

4. Write functions that perform integer division (DIV and MOD). Use them to test how your compiler handles situations involving integer division by negative values. Use various combinations of positive and negative integers and examine the output. Do these values seem to make sense?

5. Explain why it is a good idea to have precedence rules. Are there any disadvantages to the precedence scheme in Oberon?

6. Explain how a function that returns a BOOLEAN result might be useful.

7. Write a function that returns the average of three real numbers.

8. Reimplement the following procedures as functions (from chapter 4 exercises):

    a.   Subtract and Multiply.

b.   Conversion from stellar distances measured in light years to miles.

c.   Conversion from seconds to hours.

d.   Conversion from minutes to seconds.

e.   Conversion from Fahrenheit to Celsius (C = 5/9*(F − 32)).

f.   Conversion from Celsius temperature to Fahrenheit (F = 9/5*C + 32).

g.   Conversion from a fractional value to a decimal one.

9.   Use the standard procedures MAX and MIN to determine the maximum and minimum values on your system for the numeric types.

Chapter 7
The FOR Statement

7.1   The FOR Loop

One of the things that computers do very well is execute repetitious tasks. That is, actions that are done over and over again—possibly with some slight variation each time through the "loop." Statements that make actions repeat are called **loops**. Another word that means the same as looping is **iteration**.

Oberon has four different statements that provide looping. This chapter presents the first type of loop—the FOR loop. There is also a fifth way to loop (recursion), which we will discuss in a later chapter.

```
MODULE OfeFor;

(* To demonstrate how to use a FOR statement *)

    IMPORT Out;

    PROCEDURE Sum*;
    (* Notice that, just for fun, I didn't name my procedure
       'Do' as in previous examples.
       This procedure adds together the numbers 1 through 10
       and displays their sum *)
       VAR i, sum: INTEGER;
    BEGIN
        sum := 0;
        FOR i := 1 TO 10 DO
            sum := sum + i;
        END;   (* FOR *)
        Out.String("The sum of 1 through 10 is ");
        Out.Int(sum, 0); Out.Ln
    END Sum;

END OfeFor.
```

After compiling OfeFor, run OfeFor.Sum. You should get the following output,

```
The sum of 1 to 10 is 55
```

The FOR statement in procedure Sum is,

```
FOR i := 1 TO 10 DO
```

All the statements between the reserved word DO and the reserved word END will be executed over and over again, in sequence, an exact number of times.

A FOR loop can contain any number of statements, but the entire sequence is repeated as a whole. In this case, there is one statement that is executed 10 times,

```
sum := sum + i;
```

What does this statement do? It takes the value of the variable sum and adds the value of i to it, and then assigns the result back to sum. This is a method often used by programmers. A variable like sum is sometimes called a *running total* or *accumulator*. Be sure to initialize an accumulator before entering a loop.

The variable i is a **counter variable** —it keeps track of the number of times through the loop. In this case, the counter i will be given the value 1 the first time through the loop. The value '1' is the *initial value*. Because we didn't specify anything otherwise, i gets incremented by 1 each time through the loop—that is, 1 is added to it each time. So, it gets 2, then 3, then 4, and so on up to and including 10. The '10' is the *limit value*.

7.2   Details of the FOR Statement

The general form of the FOR statement is,

```
FOR <counter variable> := <initial value> TO <limit value>
BY <increment value> DO
   <sequence of statements>
END
```

The BY <increment value> is optional. If it is left out, BY 1 is assumed as the default value (this is what happened in OfeFor).

The <initial value> and <limit value> can be any expression that evaluates to an integer. Thus they can be variables, constants, functions, literals, or arithmetic expressions—as long as they evaluate to integer values.

However, the <increment value> *must be a constant expression*—an expression the compiler can evaluate at compile time. The constant expression must evaluate to an integer value. Neither variables nor functions can be used in expressions for <increment value>, but expressions involving constants and literal values are permitted. Note that negative values for <increment value> are allowed.

The <counter variable> must be defined as one of SHORTINT, INTEGER, or LONGINT.

Each time through the loop, the `<counter variable>` is incremented—given the next value. When the counter exceeds the value, the loop will end.

The `<initial value>` and the `<limit value>` are evaluated when the FOR loop is first entered. If they contain expressions, they are evaluated *only once*. This means that the FOR loop executes a fixed number of times, and that number is known as soon as the loop is entered.

Beware trying to change the `<initial value>` or `<limit value>` within the loop. You are permitted to change these values, but the loop is *blind to those changes*—it will continue on as if you hadn't changed them at all,

```
begin := 1;
end := 15;
FOR n := begin TO end DO
   end := 0;
   Out.Int(n, 0); Out.Ln
END; (* FOR *)
```

How many times will this for loop execute? The answer is 15 times! Even though we change the value of end to zero each time through the loop, the `<limit value>` was determined when the loop was entered, and changing end doesn't affect it at all.

If the `<initial value>` and the `<limit value>` are the same, the FOR loop's actions will take place only once. If the `<initial value>` is greater than the `<limit value>`, the actions are skipped entirely (the opposite is true for a negative `<increment value>`).

Something else that is very important to note; within a FOR loop, the `<counter variable>` can be assigned to or changed via procedure calls. When this happens, the FOR has, in effect, lost control over the `<counter variable>`.

It is considered bad style to change this value—only the FOR loop itself should change that value. When the FOR loop is encountered, it is expected to execute a *fixed number of times*. We should only *inspect* the value that the counter holds—use it in arithmetic expressions, for example, but not change it.

Upon exiting the FOR loop, the `<counter variable>` is defined to be the value that caused the loop to end. That is, it is the next increment beyond the `<limit value>`. In the above example, after the loop ends, n has a value of 16. You may then use the `<counter variable>` as it is, or reinitialize it in order to use it again.

As a matter of style, counter variables should be defined locally to the procedure that contains the FOR loop.

The FOR loop is useful for many applications, including generating and using sequences, patterns, and tables.

7.3   Nested FOR Loops

Recall that the term *nested* means that something appears inside something else. We have nested comments, for example.

FOR loops may also be nested:

```
FOR outer := 1 TO 5 DO
   FOR inner := 2 TO 10 BY 2 DO
   . . .
   END;       (* FOR inner *)
END;  (* FOR outer *)
```

The inner loop is executed *in its entirety* each time through the outer loop. In this case, the inner loop would be executed a total of five times; each time looping through its own set of values. Notice that the inner loop is indented a level deeper than the outer loop. This helps show the nesting relationship.

Also, notice the comments supplied at the ends of each loop. This is also helpful in keeping track of which END belongs to which FOR.

It is perfectly legal—and often desirable—for the inner loop to use the value generated by the outer loop.

7.4   Exercises

1. Explain the purpose of "loops."

2. Describe the purposes of the counter variable, initial value, limit value, and increment value within the FOR statement.

3. Write out "by hand" what you would expect the output of the following set of FOR loops to be.

    ```
    VAR i, j, k: INTEGER;

    FOR i := 0 TO 9 BY 2 DO
       FOR j := 2 TO 12 BY 3 DO
          FOR k := 1 TO 5 DO
             Out.Int( i + j + k, 0 ); Out.Ln
          END; (* FOR *)
       END; (* FOR *)
    END; (* FOR *)
    ```

4. Write a procedure that accepts a six-digit integer as an argument and writes out the digits in reverse. (*Hint:* You will need to use x MOD 10 and x DIV 10.)

5. Write a procedure to write out even numbers between 0 and 100.

6.   Write a procedure that shows that the sum of the first n odd numbers is equal to square of n (i.e., $1 + 3 + 5 + .. + n = n^2$). Test this out for different values of n.

7.   Write a function that calculates x^y using repeated multiplication. You may assume x is real and y is a positive integer.

Chapter 8
The IF Statement

8.1   Making Decisions

Sometimes we want things to happen within our programs, depending on certain conditions or states that occur during execution. That is, we want to be able to make choices in our programs. When a program executes a set of statements only under certain conditions, it is called *conditional execution* or *branching*.

We need a way to test conditions and make decisions based on those conditions. The most common way to do this in Oberon is using the IF statement.

The IF statement can be used to select values, selectively run processes, route data, make decisions, and perform error checking.

```
MODULE OfeIf;
(* Demonstrates how a decision can be made *)

    IMPORT Out;

    CONST myAge = 32;

    PROCEDURE Decide*;
    (* Writes a different message depending on the value of
       myAge *)
    BEGIN
        IF myAge > 16 THEN
            Out.String("You are old enough to get a driver's");
            Out.String(" license in most of the USA.");
            Out.Ln
        ELSE
            Out.String("You're too young to drive!");
            Out.Ln
        END;  (* IF *)
    END Decide;
END OfeIf.
```

Module OfeIf provides an example of a simple decision that might be made. Is the person whose age is given old enough to get a driver's license? The *test condition* or *guarding condition* is

```
myAge > 16
```

If the condition is true (is myAge greater than 16?), then the statements that follow are executed. If it is not true, then there are other statements that are executed instead. The "otherwise" part is marked by the reserved word ELSE.

Notice the use of the reserved word END. It marks the end of the conditional part of the statement sequence.

8.2   Boolean Expressions and Relational Operators

The IF statement relies heavily on the boolean values TRUE and FALSE. Since this is an important concept, let's look into this more in depth.

A **boolean expression** is an expression that evaluates to one of two states—TRUE or FALSE. The simplest boolean expressions are the literal values TRUE and FALSE.

Relational operators also can be used to form boolean expressions,

```
=      is equal to
<      is less than
<=     is less than or equal to
>      is greater than
>=     is greater than or equal to
#      is not equal to
```

These operators can be used in expressions that make *assertions*, or claims, that are either true or false. That is, these relational operators yield a result of type BOOLEAN.

This is basically the same idea as from mathematics. Is one numeric value equal to another? Is one value greater than another?

In Oberon, we can apply relations to character and string values as well. Does a letter occur after another letter when considering the ordinal positions of ASCII characters? Strings are compared via the ASCII sequence as well. This means that case makes a difference—'red' is not equal to 'Red'.

String variables can be compared with literal strings or with other string variables. And always remember, character arrays that are to be compared must contain 0X as a terminator to indicate the end of the string.

```
3 < 5                    (* evaluates to TRUE *)

"Eric" = authorName      (* evaluates to TRUE if the
                            identifier authorName has the
                            value "Eric", otherwise it
                            evaluates to FALSE *)
```

```
letterGrade >= "C"          (* TRUE if letterGrade is
                               "C", or "D", or "E", or ...
                               *)


sum + next  #  total        (* TRUE if sum + next is
                               not equal to total *)
```

Boolean expressions are restricted to comparing operands of compatible types. Testing if the integer number 6 is equal to the string 'six' isn't allowed, for example.

Caution: When using REAL and LONGREAL values, be careful when comparing using relational operators. The *precision* with which the computer stores values is sometimes inexact. For instance,

```
(10/3) * 3
```

might be turn out to be 9.9999999 rather than 10. Therefore, we may need check *ranges of values* for real numbers, and not exact matches. Is our answer "close enough"?

```
IF (10/3) * 3 <= 10 THEN ...
```

8.3   Boolean Variables and Constants

Boolean variables can be defined, and boolean constants may be declared as well. There isn't often a need for using boolean constants; the values TRUE and FALSE are generally clear enough—and many times are more clear than defining constants that "hide" the real value.

However, boolean variables can be very useful. For example, testing a condition once and then using it later—or using it multiple times. So don't be afraid to use "auxiliary" boolean variables to help keep track of program states and conditions that have been tested.

```
VAR done: BOOLEAN;
```

Boolean values can then be assigned to boolean variables,

```
done := TRUE;
```

Boolean expressions may be also used in assignments,

```
done := errors > 0;
```

If errors is greater than 0, done is set to TRUE. Otherwise, done is FALSE. Parentheses can be used to help clarify the expression,

```
done := (errors > 0);
(* equivalent to the preceding example *)
```

Look at the following equivalent assignments, and convince yourself that they are, in fact, equivalent,

```
done := (test = TRUE);
done := test;
```

Boolean variables can, of course, be used as a guarding condition for an IF statement,

```
IF done THEN ... END;
```

8.4   Logical Boolean Operators

More complex boolean expressions can be formed using the logical operators OR, &, and ~. These help us combine boolean expressions and, when used in IF statements, test for multiple conditions.

OR forms what is known as **logical disjunction**. That is, the expression evaluates to TRUE as long as at least one of the operands is TRUE. It evaluates to FALSE only if *both* operands are FALSE.

```
p := TRUE;
q := FALSE;
IF p OR q THEN ... END;
```

This evaluates to TRUE—p is TRUE so the whole expression p OR q is TRUE.

```
p := FALSE;
IF p OR q THEN ... END;
```

Now it evaluates to FALSE—p is FALSE and q is FALSE so the whole expression p OR q is FALSE.

& (pronounced "and") forms what is known as **logical conjunction**. The expression evaluates to TRUE only if *both* operands evaluate to TRUE. If either or both operands are FALSE, the whole expression is FALSE.

```
p := TRUE;
q := FALSE;
IF p & q THEN ... END;
```

This evaluates to FALSE—q is FALSE so the whole expression p & q is FALSE.

```
q := TRUE;
IF p & q THEN ... END;
```

Now it evaluates to TRUE—p is TRUE and q is TRUE so the whole expression p & q is TRUE.

~ (pronounced "not") is known as **negation**. It reverses a boolean condition. That is, TRUE becomes FALSE, and FALSE becomes TRUE,

```
p := TRUE;
q := ~p;
```

Here q is assigned the value FALSE—that is, ~TRUE is FALSE. ~TRUE would be read "not TRUE."

```
p := ~q;
```

In this case, p is assigned the value TRUE—that is, ~FALSE is TRUE.

```
IF ~done THEN ... END;
```

"If not done" means the block will execute only if done is FALSE.

These operators apply to BOOLEAN operands and yield a BOOLEAN result. Any boolean value may be used, even that returned by a function procedure,

```
IF ~ODD(Int) THEN ... END;
```

"If not ODD" means the block will execute if Int is even.

Parentheses help clarify these more complex boolean expressions, and are in many cases required in order to have the meaning that is intended. Remember the precedence rules? Relations have the lowest precedence. For example,

```
Int > 10 & Int < 20
```

would result in a compile-time error. The compiler would think you were trying to do

```
Int > (10 & Int) < 20
```

because of Oberon's precedence rules. Recall that '&' has the same precedence as '*' or '/'. So it would be evaluated before the relational operators '>' and '<'. In order to get this to work as intended, the relations must be enclosed by parentheses,

```
(Int > 10) & (Int < 20)
```

which tests if Int is between 10 and 20.

Parentheses may also be required when combining logical operators; again, due to operator precedence. If you refer back to the precedence table, you will see that '~' has the highest precedence and 'OR' has the lowest. That is, the order of precedence is '~', '&', and then 'OR'. As usual, among operators of equal precedence, evaluation goes from left to right.

```
p OR q & r          (* the same as p OR (q & r) *)
```

If we wanted 'p OR q' to be evaluated before the '& r', then we would use parentheses to overcome the precedence order,

```
(p OR q) & r
```

Here a few other examples:

```
p & ~q              (* p & (~q) *)
p OR q OR r         (* (p OR q) OR r *)
```

8.5   Partial Evaluation

Oberon uses what is known as *partial evaluation* when dealing with logical operators. It is also sometimes called *short-circuit evaluation*. **Partial evaluation** occurs in the evaluation process of a boolean expression—as soon as the value of an expression can be determined, the evaluation ceases. That is, the entire expression might not be evaluated if it is not necessary. For example,

```
p & q
(* stops before evaluating q, if p is FALSE *)
```

If p is FALSE, then we already know the entire expression is FALSE as soon as we have evaluated p. There is no need to continue on to evaluate q.

```
p OR q
(* stops before evaluating q, if p is TRUE *)
```

If p is TRUE, then we already know the expression is TRUE as soon as we have evaluated p. There is no need to continue on to evaluate q.

A more formal definition is,

```
p & q  =>   IF p THEN q ELSE FALSE END;
p OR q =>   IF p THEN TRUE ELSE q END;
```

Partial evaluation can be helpful in certain situations. It may sometimes save us from doing something illegal,

```
IF (denominator # 0) & (numerator/denominator > 1) THEN
...
END;
```

If we tried to evaluate the expression (numerator/denominator > 1), and denominator had a value of zero, then we'd get a run-time error. Partial evaluation keeps the divide-by-zero error from occurring. The first condition can be thought of as *guarding* the second condition. This can often help to simplify program text.

The drawback to relying on partial evaluation to save us is that we have put a dependence on order into our program. This dependence may not be obvious when it is read later (by another programmer or even by the programmer who wrote it).

Whenever such a dependence is introduced into the program, you should comment the situation to make it clearer for future reference,

```
(* divide by zero guarded by partial evaluation *)
```

Or some people like to put the comment directly within the IF statement,

```
IF (denominator # 0) & (* then if *)
   (numerator/denominator > 1) THEN ... END;
```

Of course, you can always write out the dependence explicitly,

```
IF (denominator # 0) THEN
```

```
        IF (numerator/denominator > 1) THEN
          ...
        END
    END;
```

8.6   General Forms of the IF Statement

There are three basic forms the IF statement can assume. The first of these forms is useful for basic "yes/no" type choices. If the condition is true, then do something. Otherwise, don't do anything special.

```
        IF <boolean expression> THEN
          <statements>
        END;
```

The IF statement is *always* terminated with an END, even when there is only one statement in <statements> to execute.

The second form is for "either/or" choices. If the condition is true, then do something. Otherwise, do something else.

```
        IF <boolean expression> THEN
          <statements>
        ELSE
          <other statements>
        END;
```

The third form provides various alternatives. It allows for multiple tests to be checked and special processing to be done for each. Note, however, *only the first alternative that tests true will have its actions performed.* All other alternatives will then be skipped,

```
        IF <boolean expression> THEN
          <statements>
        ELSIF <2ⁿᵈ boolean expression>
          <2ⁿᵈ set of statements>
        ELSIF <3ʳᵈ boolean expression>
          <3ʳᵈ set of statements>
        ...
        ELSE
          <"default" statements>
        END;
```

In this last form, you may have as many ELSIF parts as you need, and the ELSE part is optional. You should, however, have an ELSE part in almost all situations. It is the "fall through" condition—where none of the alternatives is true.

Recall that programs are more readable if indenting is done to show grouping. This is also true in the case of the IF statement; indent to show which statements belong within each alternative.

There are situations you should consider and be careful of when using IF statements,

- Transitions or boundary conditions. Most conditions are handled, but same cases are missing.
- Impossible conditions. The conditions can never be true.
- Unavoidable conditions. The conditions are always true.

8.7   Error Checking

The standard procedures HALT and ASSERT were mentioned in an earlier chapter. Both are useful in several ways, including *program validation* and producing *traps*.

Program validation is a method of determining the correctness of your programs. By introducing assertions about the state of a program—via preconditions and postconditions—a program is validated. If done properly, they ensure that a program will not run in an invalid state.

Traps are often used as a way to capture the program state at a particular point during execution, so that a knowledgeable person can examine that state to determine what is causing an error.

Preconditions are checks done before a particular block of statements is executed. They are assumptions made about data and program state before operating on that data. Input is checked to make certain it is within the allowable values. In the case of procedures, assertions can, for example, check that the parameters are in an appropriate range of values.

Postconditions are checks done after a block of statements has executed. They can be used to check that results are as expected, and that values produced are within expected ranges. Before a procedure returns, checks can be done to assure that the procedure has performed as it should.

Let us take a closer look at traps. In many Oberon systems, traps produce the *program stack* as their output. A **program stack** is used by a computer to keep track of procedure calls and the order in which they were called. By looking at the stack, we can see which procedures have been called and what values their variables have. Here is part of the trap output generated on my system by introducing a HALT(127) statement at the end of the procedure OfeSwap.Swap:

```
Trap 127   (programmed HALT)     PC = 898C6C3DH
(00000035H)
OfeSwap.Swap
    first = 7
    second = 3
    temp = 3
```

```
OfeSwap.Do
    one = 7
    two = 3
```

This tells us that, at the time the program halted, procedure Swap was the most recently called procedure—it was at the "top" of the stack and hence at the top of the listing. The values of all local variables are shown as well. OfeSwap.Do is listed next; it called Swap. Do is waiting for Swap to end before it can finish its own processing.

If we looked at the entire output of the trap, we could see the exact order in which procedures were called to get to that point in the program—albeit they would be in reverse order.

Examining this output can be extremely helpful when attempting to debug programs. Combining IF statements with calls to HALT (or, equivalently, using ASSERT) is extremely useful in observing program behavior as "snapshots" at various points during execution.

However, you should be very careful about using HALT and ASSERT in a finished program. They should be "last ditch" alternatives. That is, most people—the *end-users* who use your programs—don't want to see the state of the program stack. They want the program to work right or, if it doesn't work right, to explain to them in plain English what has gone wrong.

This is not to say that there is no place for ASSERT and HALT in finished programs—after all the end-user might even be able to save the trap to a file or print it out, and then return it to the programmer (an excellent way for the programmer to find out what happened "after the fact").

But there are other ways of dealing with program errors. IF statements can be used to perform error checking. This helps make programs **robust**—that is, less sensitive to users' errors or misuse. That way, programs end gracefully instead of crashing.

There are a number of ways IF statements can be used to make a program more robust:

- Provide alternatives—note the error and continue. Possibly continuing along another path, such as running a different process.
- Fix the problem and continue. Or allow the user the chance to fix the error or re-enter data.
- Produce a meaningful message and then quit.

8.8   Simplifying Boolean Expressions

Dealing with multiple boolean expressions can be tricky—things can get complicated and unreadable very quickly. Using *truth tables* and a few *logic laws* can help simplify expressions.

Truth tables show the rules of how boolean operators are evaluated:

Table 8.1: Negation

~TRUE is FALSE
~FALSE is TRUE

Table 8.2: & and OR

TRUE & FALSE is FALSE	TRUE OR FALSE is TRUE
TRUE & TRUE is TRUE	TRUE OR TRUE is TRUE
FALSE & TRUE is FALSE	FALSE OR TRUE is TRUE
FALSE & FALSE is FALSE	FALSE OR FALSE is FALSE

The **distributive laws** help simplify combinations of '&' and 'OR',

Table 8.3: Distributive Laws

(p OR r) & (q OR r) = (p & q) OR r
(p & r) OR (q & r)   = (p OR q) & r

DeMorgan's laws also help with combinations involving '~',

Table 8.4: DeMorgan's Laws

(~p) & (~q) = ~(p OR q)
(~p) OR (~q) = ~(p & q)

Be careful when using combinations involving '~'. Negated expressions can be more difficult to understand because you are, in a way, thinking "backwards." DeMorgan's laws are very helpful in making certain we are doing what it is we intend to do.

8.9   Exercises

1. Decide whether the following are valid relations and then determine if they evaluate to TRUE or FALSE. Assume string = "Exercise 1", int = 8, rl = 8.0, and char = "8".

   a. `int = char`   e. `char = CHR( int )`
   b. `int = ORD( char )`   f. `char > "7"`
   c. `string < char`   g. `string # "E"`
   d. `rl >= int`   h. `int + rl = 16`

2. Assuming p, q and r are boolean variables, where p = TRUE, q = FALSE, and r = TRUE, determine whether the following expressions evaluate to TRUE or FALSE. (Make sure you take precedence into account.)

   a. `p OR q & r`   e. `q & p OR q & r`
   b. `p & q OR r`   f. `~( p & q ) OR ~r`
   c. `p & r OR q`   g. `p & ~( q OR r )`
   d. `p & ~q & r`   h. `~p OR ~q OR ~r`

3. Describe the three general forms of the IF statement and explain the purpose and use of each.

4. Describe preconditions and postconditions and explain why they help ensure that a program is correct.

5. Introduce a call to HALT into one of your modules and see how your system responds to program termination.

6. Write a procedure that will write out a four-digit integer in words.

7. Write a procedure that is passed a string and writes out occurrences of double letters. Then change it so that it also recognizes occurrences of triple letters.

8. Write a procedure that is passed three integers and determines which is the smallest. Then a procedure that determines which is largest.

9. Write a procedure that is passed three integers and sorts them from smallest to largest.

10. Using only In.Char; write a procedure that works just like In.Int.

11. Write a procedure that is passed a string and replaces all tab characters with a fixed number of spaces.

12. Write your own versions of the standard procedures ABS and ENTIER.

Chapter 9
Other Looping Statements

9.1 Looping Statements

There are three looping statements discussed in this section: WHILE, REPEAT, and LOOP. Oberon has many different types of looping statements for a reason. Each one is tailored to specific situations and makes those situations easier to read, write, and understand.

Could Oberon have been designed with fewer types of looping statements? The answer is yes, it could have. However, having multiple types can make the programmer's intentions more clear. A FOR loop, for example, is expected to execute a fixed number of times. Someone reading the source text should find the loop easier to understand with this prior knowledge.

In this chapter, we will see where the other types of loops fit in.

9.2 The WHILE Loop

Suppose we wanted to read in a list of numbers and add them all together. Sounds like a looping job—read a number, add it to the running total, and do it again until you run out of numbers.

Why not use FOR, as we did before? Remember, when we use a FOR loop, we need to know beforehand how many times we are going to repeat the loop. With WHILE, however, we don't. Here is a variation on OfeFor,

```
MODULE OfeSumnums;

(* Demonstrate use of while statement to sum numbers *)

   IMPORT In, Out;
```

```
PROCEDURE Sum*;
(* read in real values and total them *)
   VAR realInput, total: REAL;
BEGIN
   In.Open;
   total := 0;
   (* remember to initialize the accumulator *)
   In.Real(realInput);
   WHILE In.Done DO
      total := total + realInput;
      In.Real(realInput)
   END;  (* WHILE *)
   Out.String("The sum of the read numbers is ");
   Out.Real(total, 0); Out.Ln
END Sum;
```

END OfeSumnums.

If we execute the command OfeReadnums.Sum on the following data:

```
21 22 20.5 23.75 23.25 31.0 457.15 60 5.3 2.2 11
```

we get this output:

```
The total sum of the read numbers is 677.15
```

After opening the input via In.Open and initializing `total` to 0, the first number is read using In.Real. The WHILE loop is then entered.

The WHILE statement is a little different from FOR; instead of keeping track of the number of times through the loop, the WHILE simply tests a boolean condition, similar to the IF statement. If the WHILE condition is TRUE, the loop executes. If the condition is FALSE, the loop ends.

In this case, the condition is a boolean variable `In.Done`. Recall that `In.Done` is set to TRUE when In.Open has succeeded in finding a place from which to get input.

If the input operation `In.Real` succeeds, In.Done remains TRUE. When we run out of input (or have invalid input), In.Done is set to FALSE. In this way, we can read as many numbers as we need to—and have a way to determine when we are finished reading them.

Why did we have to call In.Real once before entering the WHILE loop? For two reasons: to initialize `realInput` and to make sure we have valid numbers to read. If In.Real was unable to read a number (and In.Done was set to FALSE), then the WHILE loop wouldn't have been executed even once.

That is an important thing to remember about WHILE loops: they may not execute their statements at all. Basically, you can think of WHILE as having an *entry condition*. If the condition isn't met the first time it is encountered, the loop is skipped entirely.

The general form of the WHILE statement is:

```
WHILE <boolean expression is TRUE> DO
   <sequence of statements>
END
```

9.3   The REPEAT Loop

The REPEAT loop is very similar to WHILE, but there are two significant differences. The first is that REPEAT is unavoidable; that is, it is guaranteed to execute its statements at least once.

The second is that the REPEAT has an *exit condition*—you are in the loop until some condition is met. Contrast this to the WHILE's entry condition, you can't enter (or re-enter) a WHILE loop unless the condition is met.

The following example is slightly more complicated than the examples we have been doing, but it shows the need for error checking in our programs. Recall that a *prime number* is a positive integer that is evenly divisible only by 1 and the number itself. Thus the numbers 1, 2, 3, 5, 7, 11, 13, 17, 19, 23... are prime; whereas 4, 6, 8, 9, 10, 12, 14, 15, 16... are not.

```
MODULE OfePrimes;

(* Read a number, and then print out whether it is prime or
not *)

   IMPORT In, Out;

   PROCEDURE IsPrime(num: INTEGER): BOOLEAN;
   (* Returns TRUE if num is prime, and FALSE otherwise *)
      VAR   divisor, remainder: INTEGER;
   BEGIN
      remainder := 0;
      (* a simple way to test for "primeness" *)
      IF num > 0 THEN
         divisor := 2;            (* start with 2 *)
         REPEAT
            remainder := num MOD divisor;
            divisor := divisor + 1
         UNTIL (remainder = 0) OR (divisor >= num)
      (* and test all integers up to num *)
      END;  (* IF *)
      RETURN (remainder # 0)
   END IsPrime;
```

```
PROCEDURE Do*;
   VAR input: INTEGER;
BEGIN
   In.Open;
   In.Int(input);
   IF In.Done THEN
   (* What does this first IF check for? *)
      Out.Int(input, 0);
      IF IsPrime(input) THEN
         Out.String(" is prime.")
      ELSE
         Out.String(" is NOT prime.")
      END;      (* IF *)
   ELSE
      Out.String("Invalid input: can't read number")
   END;  (* IF *)
   Out.Ln;
END Do;
```

```
END OfePrimes.
```

Can you see where we have done error checking? After you have read OfePrimes and compiled it, try different values as input; run it several times with different values. Try using 0 or a negative number as input. What happens? How about when a real number is used for input?

The procedure OfePrimes.Do reads an input value and then attempts to determine whether that value is a prime number or not. The statement

```
IF In.Done THEN
```

is how we check the input. It is a *precondition* for continuing with the rest of the command. If we haven't read a valid input value, then an error message is displayed in the log.

The next statement of interest is

```
IF IsPrime(input) THEN
```

IsPrime is a function procedure; a call to it forms a boolean expression that we can use as part of the IF statement. The function is invoked, and returns a value of either TRUE or FALSE, depending on the value of its argument.

IsPrime uses a brute force method of determining whether a number is prime. "Brute force" means that we are going to check every single value possible until we find one that works. Let us look at this function more closely.

After initializing remainder—which we will use to keep track of the remainder value—we have another precondition to check:

```
IF num > 0 THEN
```

Is the number we are testing for "primeness" greater than 0? Recall that a prime must be a positive integer—if the number is 0, or less than 0, we don't need to bother continuing because the number has already failed the test for "primeness."

```
divisor := 2;
```

The value of `divisor` is initialized to 2, which is the first number we want to try. Then we enter into the loop:

```
REPEAT
    remainder := num MOD divisor;
    divisor := divisor + 1
UNTIL (remainder = 0) OR (divisor >= num)
```

We use the MOD operator to get the remainder. If num divides evenly by `divisor`, the remainder is 0. Then we increment the value we want to check. That is important to remember in loops other than FOR—only FOR automatically increments counters; we have to do it explicitly in other kinds of loops.

Now we have reached the UNTIL part of the repeat loop. UNTIL marks our exit condition. In this case, we have a *compound exit condition*. If we have found a number that divides evenly (remainder = 0) then we might as well stop—the number isn't prime.

What about the next condition? Why do we need to check `divisor >= num`? Because we want to stop after we have checked all the possible values.

So, one way or another, our loop ends. Either we have found a value that gives remainder of 0, or we have run out of values to check. Now, how do we convey this information back to the point where IsPrime was called?

```
RETURN (remainder # 0)
```

Look back carefully at the body of IsPrime. Does this makes sense? We have set up the procedure so that `remainder` keeps track of whether we have found a prime. It is initialized to 0 at the beginning of the procedure, so that if nothing else happens, we can say that the number passed is not prime (remainder # 0 would evaluate to FALSE).

Every time through the REPEAT loop, `remainder` becomes the current remainder. If it never gets set back to 0 by the MOD operation (we never find a remainder of zero), then num is prime (remainder # 0 is TRUE).

Could we have written the loop as a WHILE? Yes, that is entirely possible.

```
remainder := 1;
WHILE (remainder # 0) & (divisor < num) DO
    remainder := num MOD divisor;
    divisor := divisor + 1
END (* WHILE *)
```

Actually, we should probably rewrite the whole procedure if we decide we would rather use a WHILE (we could potentially do away with the precondition error checking). However, the point of the example is to show that REPEAT and WHILE are very similar statements. You can always rewrite one as the other.

Note that when rewriting a REPEAT as a WHILE, we had to reverse the conditions—make exit conditions into entry conditions. Also, we had to make sure there was a way to get into the loop the first time (setting `remainder := 1`, before the WHILE).

The general form of REPEAT is:

```
REPEAT
    <sequence of statements>
UNTIL <boolean expression is TRUE>
```

9.4   The LOOP Statement

Sometimes, WHILE and REPEAT are less than adequate for our needs. What happens if our exit condition should be tested in the middle of the loop? What if we have several different exit conditions?

The LOOP statement is at the same time both more general and more basic than the other types of loops. A sequence of statements is executed until an exit condition is met.

The following is a simple example:

```
MODULE OfeCountch;
(* Counts the number of characters input *)

    IMPORT In, Out;

    PROCEDURE Count*;
    (* Reads characters one at time and counts them *)
        VAR count: INTEGER; ch: CHAR;
    BEGIN
        In.Open;
        count := 0;
        LOOP
            In.Char(ch);
            IF ~In.Done THEN EXIT END;
            INC(count)
        END;   (* LOOP *)
        Out.Int(count, 0);
        Out.String(" characters read."); Out.Ln
    END Count;

END OfeCountch.
```

OfeCountch.Count counts the characters in a selection of text (note that nonprinted characters such as tab are also counted). After initializations, we enter the loop where a character is read. Then,

```
IF ~In.Done THEN EXIT END;
```

forms the exit condition. The EXIT statement causes the loop to be departed immediately. It is normally found within an IF statement, as it is here. If the IF statement's guarding condition is satisfied, then the EXIT causes execution to resume with the next statement following the END of the LOOP. You generally don't want to have an ELSE part in this type of exit condition—it is legal to do so, but it can make your loop more confusing.

The LOOP, in this case, is even simpler than the equivalent WHILE would be:

```
In.Char(ch);
WHILE In.Done DO
    INC(count);
    In.Char(ch)
END;   (* WHILE *)
```

With WHILE, we would have to call In.Char(ch) once before the loop—to ensure that there is at least one character able to be read—and then again within the loop to read any remaining characters.

Some people like to place an empty comment '(**)' in front of the exit condition(s) in order to help locate it in the source text,

```
(**)IF ~In.Done THEN EXIT END;
```

The general form of the loop statement is:

```
LOOP
    <sequence of statements with at least one EXIT>
END
```

9.5   Looping Guidelines

Let us consider again the reasons why Oberon has so many different types of loops. The foremost reason is that statements should help programmers accomplish their goals clearly and correctly. So, each type of loop is tailored to fit a specific situation.

The FOR loop is used when a loop is to be executed a fixed number of times and that information is known at the beginning of the loop. The FOR has the advantage that the counter is automatically incremented.

The WHILE loop is used when the condition should be checked before the loop is executed even once. The WHILE's statements may not be executed at all, depending on whether the entry condition is met.

The REPEAT loop is used when the statements *must* execute at least one time. The REPEAT always executes its statements at least once.

The LOOP is the most general loop statement. It should be used when there are several potential exit conditions or when the exit conditions are in the middle of the loop.

Remember that REPEAT and LOOP have exit conditions; WHILE has an entry condition.

Any situation requiring looping can be expressed by any one of these types—it is just that usually one type of loop is easier and clearer than the other types for that situation. Many times, "easier and clearer" is a very subjective determination. From my own observations of various sources, the WHILE loop seems to be the most common type of loop used by Oberon programmers. This is not to say that WHILE is most often the best choice, but rather that programmers have gotten "used to" using it, and therefore tend to write almost everything in that style.

LOOP has some advantages over WHILE and REPEAT. The programmer has more control over how and when the loop is ended and exit conditions. This can often simplify the loop, as we did in OfeCountch. Exit conditions are often easier to understand than entry conditions—"Keep going until this occurs," rather than, "As long as this condition holds, keep going."

Basically, what this all means is that it is up to you to decide what type of loop is best to use in a given situation. You have four tools available, and you have to judge when it is best to use each one.

Try to write loops as WHILE or FOR first. If it turns out that what you want to do is too cumbersome using either of these, then look at LOOP or REPEAT.

Be cautious when using any type of loop. Make sure that it is possible to meet the exit condition (or in the case of entry conditions, that it is possible to *not* meet it). Otherwise, you might have an **infinite loop**—a loop that never ends. FOR is usually the safest in this respect; although if you change the value of the counter variable within the FOR, you may still end up with an infinite loop. That is why it is generally considered bad style to change the value of the counter in a FOR loop.

Be careful of exit (and entry) condition bugs—review boolean conditions and the IF statement. Keep conditions as simple as possible.

9.6 Debugging Statements

Looping statement bugs are a common source of errors. Infinite loops and other exit condition bugs are sometimes difficult to find without knowing what is happening within the loop at run-time.

A common way to help trace the source of the problem is to use operations from module Out to examine values. For example,

```
In.Real(input);
WHILE In.Done DO
    In.Real(input);
    Out.Real(input, 0); Out.Ln;
    total := total + input
END;  (* WHILE *)
```

Can you spot the error in this loop? If we want to sum a list of numbers, there are two problems, which become obvious if we execute this loop with the embedded Out procedures. For the input,

```
12 2.5 3.75 3.0 1.3 4.15 6
```

we get the output,

```
2.5
3.75
3.0
1.3
4.15
6.0
6.0
```

Can you see the error now? The way the loop is written, the first number (12) is skipped and the last number (6) is added twice. The corrected WHILE loop is

```
In.Real(input);
WHILE In.Done DO
    Out.Real(input, 0); Out.Ln;
    total := total + input;
    In.Real(input)
END;    (* WHILE *)
```

Using procedures from Out allows us to examine a "moving picture" of execution. We discussed using traps during a debugging session before, but they don't allow the full execution of the loop to be seen. Traps are "snapshots" at a particular point, and although they are very useful, examining the values as they change throughout execution is often more useful.

9.7   Exercises

1. Explain the differences and similarities between WHILE, REPEAT, and LOOP.

2. Describe what entry and exit conditions are and how they relate to looping statements.

3. Write a procedure that will write out numbers with commas in the right places.

4. Write a procedure that is passed two integers and uses them as operands to a multiplication problem that is written out as if it were done by hand.

5. Write procedures similar to In.Int and Out.Int to read in and write out fractional numbers written in the form a/b (for example, "1/2").

6. Write a procedure that is passed a string and converts it to all uppercase letters using WHILE. Then rewrite it to use REPEAT, and then LOOP.

7. Introduce debugging statements into your procedures from exercises 3 to 6 so that you can "watch" your loop's progress.

8. Rewrite the following using FOR, REPEAT, and then LOOP:

```
i := 100;
k := 0;
WHILE i > 0 DO
    i := i DIV 2;
    INC(k)
END; (* WHILE *)
```

9. Explain which kind of loop is the "best" way of writing exercise 8. Give details as to why you think so.

10. Write a procedure that will write out a calendar for a whole year. Give appropriate headings for months and days.

Chapter 10
The CASE Statement

10.1 Choosing Alternatives

Although we could use IF for all situations involving conditional execution—that is, making decisions or choosing alternatives—Oberon provides another statement that helps to simplify certain situations. For instance, suppose we wanted to count the number of vowels in a text selection:

```
MODULE OfeCase;
(* Count the vowels in a text selection *)

    IMPORT In, Out;

    PROCEDURE Count*;
    (* Read characters. Keep track of how many are vowels *)
        VAR countVowels: INTEGER; ch: CHAR;
    BEGIN
        In.Open;
        countVowels := 0;
        LOOP
            In.Char(ch);
            (**)IF ~In.Done THEN EXIT END;
            CASE ch OF
                    "a", "e", "i", "o", "u",
                    "A", "E", "I", "O", "U": INC(countVowels)
            ELSE
            END;        (* CASE *)
        END;  (* LOOP *)
        Out.Int(countVowels, 0);
        Out.String(" vowels read."); Out.Ln;
    END Count;
END OfeCase.
```

This is very similar to OfeCountch, except that within the loop, we want to count only vowels. We could have used an IF statement:

```
IF ch = "a" OR ch = "e" OR ch = "i" OR
    ch = "o" OR ch = "u" OR ch = "A" OR
    ch = "E" OR ch = "I" OR ch = "O" OR
    ch = "U" THEN
      INC(countVowels)
END;
```

But in this situation, CASE is more straightforward. CASE allows us to list *distinct alternatives* and the actions that go with each alternative.

10.2 The CASE Statement

The general form of the CASE statement is,

```
CASE <case expression> OF
    <1st label list>: <1st set of statements>
 |  <2nd label list>: <2nd set of statements>
 . . .
 |  <last label list>: <last set of statements>
ELSE
    <default statements>
END
```

First the `<case expression>` is evaluated, and then its type is determined. The case expression can be any integer type or have type CHAR.

After the value of the case expression is evaluated, that value is matched against the case labels. The **case labels** represent potential values of the case expression. A vertical bar (' | ') separates each set of labels and statements.

If the value of the case expression matches one of the labels, the corresponding set of statements is executed. The first match is the only one whose statements are executed; the CASE then terminates—execution continues with the statement after the END.

If there is no match in any of the label lists, the statements following the ELSE are used. If there is no ELSE part, and the case expression cannot be matched with any case label, it is considered an error; this normally produces a trap.

Note that the type of the case expression must be compatible with the type of the labels. You can't have an integer case expression with character case labels. The case expression is usually a variable.

Case labels must be constants or literal values; they cannot be variables or expressions involving variables or functions. Constant expressions can be used; that is, an expression that involves only constants (and can thus be evaluated at compile time). No value in the case label list can occur more than once.

Empty statements are allowed to follow a case label. And two or more labels can initiate the same set of actions by grouping—either as a comma-separated list of labels or by using a range ('..'). The '..' means "through and including." For example,

```
CASE ch OF
    "a" .. "z": LowerCaseOp(ch); INC(countLC)
|   "A" .. "Z": UpperCaseOp(ch); INC(countUC)
|   "0" .. "9": DigitOp(ch); INC(countDigits)
|   ".", "!", "?":
ELSE
    otherOp(ch); INC(countOther)
END;
```

In this example, lower-case letters get processed one way, upper case letters another way, digits are handled a third way, and ".", "!", and "?" are just skipped with no special processing. The ELSE is provided to allow for all other choices. Remember, if the case expression can't match any of the labels, it is an error. So you should always provide an ELSE part—even if it doesn't do anything (although error processing would be preferable).

When should you use CASE instead of IF? Case labels can be easier to use than boolean expressions for describing groups or ranges of values; the alternative actions are often easier to see.

Case alternatives are truly mutually exclusive. The compiler will not allow any label to be repeated; so order doesn't matter, as it might using ELSIF. Also, ELSIF may unintentionally overlap ranges.

10.3 Exercises

1. Describe the advantages and disadvantages of using case statements.

2. Explain why you think only integer and character values are permitted as case expressions. Why not real values?

3. Explain errors and other potential problems with the following:

```
CASE expr OF
    ODD(expr): INC(oddCount)
|   2 .. 100 : INC(evenCount)
|   3.14, 1  : INC(otherCount)
|   3        : INC(threeCount)
END; (* CASE *)
```

4. Write a procedure to convert a grade point to a letter grade. Allow for letter grades with "+" and "–". (For example, 3.8 to 4.0 is A+, 3.5 to 3.7 is A, 3.2 to 3.4 is A–,

etc.). Can you use CASE to make decisions in this situation? If so, what assumptions/ decisions must you make?

5. Write functions IsDigit(), IsAlpha(), IsAlphaNum(), and IsUpper(). All are passed a single character and return boolean results with the following values:

    a. IsDigit() returns true if the character is a digit. False otherwise.
    b. IsAlpha() returns true if the character is a letter. False otherwise.
    c. IsAlphaNum() returns true if the character is a digit or a letter. False otherwise.
    d. IsUpper() returns true if the character is an uppercase letter. False otherwise.

6. Write your own versions of the standard procedures CAP, CHR, and ORD.

Part II

Types

Chapter 11
Working with Types

11.1   What Is a Type?

Type describes data and defines what operations are permitted on values. Type information helps the compiler decide which values can be assigned to variables.

The **type declaration** binds an identifier to properties of the object that it represents. In Oberon, the declared properties are *constant* and valid within the scope of the identifier. That is, although the value of a variable may change, its declared properties remain the same throughout the time of its existence.

In Oberon, *everything* has a type: literal values, constants, variables, expressions, functions, and even procedures. That is what makes Oberon a *strongly typed language*—the compiler checks the type of each object and verifies that it is used appropriately.

Variables are *instances* of a type. When the variable is defined, enough computer memory is allocated so that the variable can hold values of the type it represents. You can have as many variables of the same type as you need; but the type itself is unique. You declare a type only once.

Type defines the *structure of the data* and what we can do with that data. For instance, integer values are stored in computer memory differently than real values, and integer division is different from real division.

The concept of type is beneficial in a number of ways. It can help reduce programmer errors, and can make programs more efficient. Type also helps reduce program complexity and clarify the meaning of programs.

11.2   Defining New Types

Basic types—INTEGER, CHAR, REAL, and so forth—are not always sufficient for our programming needs. As we proceed, we will learn how to declare types that may suit our needs much better.

Let us begin by declaring a string type,

```
MODULE OfeType;

(* Demonstrates how to declare a new type *)

    IMPORT In, Out;

    TYPE
        String = ARRAY 80 OF CHAR;
        (* The new type has the name String. Its structure is
            an array of characters *)

    PROCEDURE Echo*;
    (* Declare a variable of type String and use it to echo a
        selection to the log *)
        VAR str: String;
    BEGIN
        In.Open;
        LOOP
            In.String(str);
            (**)IF ~In.Done THEN EXIT END;
            Out.String(str); Out.Ln;
        END;  (* LOOP *)

    END Echo;

END OfeType.
```

The command OfeType.Echo applied to the selection,

```
"hello world" "testing 123" "Last"
```

produces the following output,

```
hello world
testing 123
Last
```

Notice that we have used the reserved word TYPE in the module to indicate we want to declare a new type. Types are usually declared in a module after CONST declarations and before procedure declarations. This is what we did in OfeType:

```
    TYPE
        String = ARRAY 80 OF CHAR;
```

Declaring String in this way gives us the ability to define variables of type String. So in procedure Echo,

```
    VAR str: String;
```

Now we can use the variable `str` just as we would a variable defined as type ARRAY 80 OF CHAR.

What advantages did declaring a type String give us? It saves us the bother of having to type in "ARRAY 80 OF CHAR" every time. But other than that, we haven't gained very much. We will see in the following chapters how to declare more useful types.

The idea we will explore is the ability to create **structured types**—a type built up from smaller pieces and having some sort of internal structure. We use basic types to build structured types. There are two kinds of structured types in Oberon: ARRAY and RECORD types are built from elements of basic types.

11.3   Type Compatibility and Named Typing

We have already talked about how, in Oberon, most types are incompatible. For example, you cannot use a character value as an operand in real division and you cannot assign a string value to an integer variable.

Oberon uses **named typing**—types are identical only if they have the same name within the same scope. For example,

```
TYPE
    String = ARRAY 80 OF CHAR;
    Name   = ARRAY 80 OF CHAR;
```

`String` and `Name` have different names, which makes them different types, and are thus incompatible. If we defined variables of these types,

```
VAR
    str: String; nm: Name;
```

The following assignment would be illegal:

```
str := nm;   (* ERROR! Incompatible types *)
```

Even though `str` and `nm` have exactly the same structure, they cannot be directly assigned to one another.

In Oberon, type compatibility is based on the names of the types (name equivalence) rather than the structure of the types (structure equivalence). There are very restricted ways in which types with different names are compatible. We have seen the compatibility of numeric types, and will see later on several more situations in which types with different names are compatible.

As a general rule, however, types are compatible only if they have the same name within the same scope.

11.4 Exercises

1. Describe the meaning of type and why it is important.

2. Describe the differences between types and variables.

3. Explain how new types are declared and describe the compatibility limitations of these types.

4. Write a procedure that defines variables of types String and Name.

    ```
    TYPE

        String = ARRAY 80 OF CHAR:
        Name   = ARRAY 80 OF CHAR;
    ```

    Try to discover a way to copy a value from a String variable to a Name variable. (*Hint*: Look at Oberon's standard procedures.) Why do you think this "loophole" exists?

5. Write a boolean function IsProper(), which is passed a fraction (numerator and denominator) and returns true if it is a proper fraction.

6. Write a procedure that calculates the sum of two fractions. (*Hint*: a/b + c/d = (ad + bc) / (bd).)

7. The procedures in exercises 5 and 6 both deal with fractions. But each fraction needs to be treated as two separate pieces—a numerator and a denominator. Do you think it would be a good idea to be able to "group together" these two pieces into one entity? Explain your answer and give possible advantages of such a "grouping" facility.

Chapter 12
Array Types

12.1 Using Arrays

We have been using one kind of array for quite a while now—ARRAY OF CHAR. But so far, a lot of the details have been left out about what it means to be an array.

An **array** is an ordered sequence of values. As with everything in Oberon, each of those values has a type. Within an array, all values must be of the same type. Arrays are one of the structured types—they have a definite internal structure.

The following is an example showing how to manipulate the elements of an array. In this case, an ARRAY OF CHAR,

```
MODULE OfeArray;

(* Read in a selection, then write it out in reverse *)

   IMPORT In, Out;

   CONST
      maxLength = 256;

   TYPE
      String = ARRAY maxLength OF CHAR;

   PROCEDURE Reverse*;
   (* Notice there are actually two loops within this
      procedure. Why? *)
      VAR str: String; length, i: INTEGER;
   BEGIN
      In.Open;
      length := 0;
      In.String(str);
      WHILE str[length] # 0X DO INC(length) END;

      FOR i := length - 1 TO 0 BY -1 DO
```

```
        Out.Char(str[i])
    END;    (* FOR *)
    Out.Ln
END Reverse;

END OfeArray.
```

For the input,

`"A string to reverse"`

you should get the output,

`esrever ot gnirts A`

Within the procedure Reverse, we define a variable of type String, and then read in a string value using In.String. (*Caution*: Because of maxLength, if you try to read in a string longer than 255 characters, you'll probably generate a trap in In.String.) The next line,

```
WHILE str[length] # 0X DO INC(length) END;
```

is used to figure out how many characters were read. In.String *automatically* marks the end of the string—it sets the character following the last one read to 0X (the string terminating character). In this way, we can tell where the string "ends." At the end of this WHILE loop, length holds the length of the string.

The new notation here is str[length]. We know that str is a variable whose type is ARRAY 256 OF CHAR—each element is a CHAR. These elements are *ordered*, so we can look at a particular element by specifying a *subscript* or *index*, which indicates the location of the element in the sequence.

That is, to get at the first CHAR in str, the index is 0 (programmers like to start numbering at 0 rather than 1—it's something you'll just have to get used to).

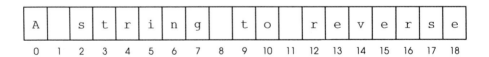

We associate the index with the array variable by using square brackets [ ]. The value held in the first element of str (str[0]) is 'A'. The next element, str[1] is a space ' '. The third, str[2] is 's' and so on.

The element str[19] holds the string terminator 0X. But we don't have to stop there. We can access each element, up to and including the last element in the array—in this case, str[255].

The index must be an integer type, which means it can be a literal, constant, variable, function, or expression, which evaluates to any of the integer types. In OfeArray, we used the variables length and i as indices.

The FOR loop in Reverse writes out each element starting at str[length − 1] and then moving backwards through each element. We don't start at str[length] because indices always start at 0, and so we have to subtract 1 from the length to get the actual position of the last character. This example shows something of the *random access* nature of arrays; that is, we can look at the elements in any order we choose.

12.2 Why Use Arrays?

Arrays are good for holding a lot of information. The information is held in an ordered manner, so we can represent things like strings, in which the order is important. Also we can move elements from one position to another—rearrange their order—and thus perform sorting of values.

When using arrays, we don't need to name each variable individually. Only the array as a whole needs to be named. Each element is then "named" individually and uniquely by the array name and the position (i.e., index) that the element has in the array.

As was mentioned before, arrays are random access structures. We can look at values in any order we want.

Character strings, or "texts," are a major application of arrays. A natural model of text is an ordered sequence of characters.

12.3 Details of Arrays

An **array** is a structured data type that represents a set of elements that are *all of the same type*. The number of elements is fixed and is called the array's *length*. The name of an array variable refers to all of its elements. An individual member is identified with a number called the index. Indices are integers between 0 and the length of the array minus one.

Array variables cannot be compared using relational operators. The exception is the type ARRAY n OF CHAR (we have already seen examples of comparing string values).

Array declarations need to specify the type of the elements. Elements can be basic types (CHAR, INTEGER, REAL, etc.) or structured types—including other arrays.

Array elements may themselves be arrays. An *array of arrays* is called a **multidimensional array**. A "normal" array—with only one dimension or row—is called a one-dimensional array.

```
TYPE
    tableType = ARRAY 3 OF ARRAY 3 OF INTEGER;
```

What does `tableType` represent? As the name implies, it can be thought of as a table. If we defined a variable t of type tableType, each entry in the table could be accessed as shown below.

	0	1	2
0	t(0, 0)	t(0, 1)	t(0, 2)
1	t(1, 0)	t(1, 1)	t(1, 2)
2	t(2, 0)	t(2, 1)	t(2, 2)

For each entry in the table, you need a "row" and "column" index. The type table-Type is called a *two-dimensional array*. There is a "shorthand" way of defining multidimensional arrays; the following declaration is equivalent to the previous declaration of tableType,

```
TYPE
    tableType = ARRAY 3, 3 OF INTEGER;
```

There are also two different, equivalent notations for indexing multidimensional arrays. We have already seen the form a[n1, n2, ...]. The other form is a[n1][n2]... So, t[1, 2] can be written t[1][2]. The reason for this has to do with the fact that multidimensional arrays are arrays of arrays. Both notations mean the same thing and are interchangeable.

What would happen if we tried to access an invalid element, say t[4, 5]? This would cause an array *out-of-bounds error* at run-time. That is, it would cause a trap. The **bounds** of an array are the first and last valid subscripts of an array dimension. For Oberon, the lower bound is always 0. The upper bound is always the length of the dimension minus 1.

Because accessing subscripts outside of those bounds doesn't make any sense, Oberon deals with bounds violations as run-time errors—which generally produce a trap and end the program. These are also known as *range errors*.

The predeclared procedure LEN can be used to find the length of each dimension. Assume VAR length: INTEGER,

```
TYPE
    String = ARRAY 32 OF CHAR;
    (* one-dimensional array of CHAR *)

    A3D = ARRAY 6, 5, 4 OF REAL;
    (* three-dimensional array of REAL *)
    ...

    length := LEN(String);
    (* length = 32, could have used LEN(String, 0) *)
    length := LEN(A3D, 0);
    (* length = 6, could have used LEN(A3D) *)

    length := LEN(A3D, 1);   (* length = 5 *)
    length := LEN(A3D, 2);   (* length = 4 *)
```

Multidimensional array types can have as many dimensions as the implementation will allow.

The general form of an array declaration is:

```
ARRAY <length(s) of dimensions> OF <type>
```

The length is actually optional; arrays declared without length are called **open arrays**. We have already used open arrays as formal parameters, but array types may also be declared as open arrays.

```
TYPE
    RealArray = ARRAY OF REAL;
```

There are restrictions on the use of open arrays, and we will talk about them in more depth in a later section.

When the length is present, it must be known at compile time. That is, it has to be a literal, constant, or constant expression. In declarations of multidimensional arrays, lengths are separated by commas.

Let us examine another example:

```
TYPE A1 = ARRAY 10 OF INTEGER;

VAR a: A1;
    b: ARRAY 10 OF INTEGER;
```

The variable b has an **anonymous type**—there is no name associated with the type of b. Because of Oberon's name equivalence rule, b is not type-compatible with a, even though they both have the same structure.

12.4 Array Assignment

Assignments to arrays can be done in two different ways: element-by-element or all elements at once. In either case, array elements must be compatible types.

Indices are used for element-by-element assignment. Elements are then assigned one at a time,

```
otherArr[1] := oneArr[0];
```

The first element of oneArr is assigned to the second element of otherArr.

Individual array elements can be assigned within loops; in this next example, assume that the elements of destination are assignment compatible with source, *and* destination is large enough to hold all the elements of source. If we want to copy all the elements of one array to the other,

```
FOR i := 0 TO LEN(source) - 1 DO
    destination[i] := source[i]
END
```

```
(* Note the use of LEN() to find the length of the array *)
```

Because each element is dealt with individually, the arrays themselves don't have to be of the same type, as long as the *elements* are assignment compatible. We could still use this same FOR loop even if the variables were defined as,

```
VAR
      destination: ARRAY 20 OF REAL;
      source:      ARRAY 10 OF INTEGER;
```

The type of source[i] is INTEGER; we are referring to a particular element. And destination[i] has type REAL. Recall that an integer variable may be assigned to a real variable.

The following is another, slightly more complex, example:

```
VAR
    twoD:   ARRAY 3, 4 OF INTEGER;
    threeD: ARRAY 4, 5, 6 OF INTEGER;
    . . .

threeD[1, 2, 3] := twoD[2, 1];
(* INTEGER assigned to INTEGER *)
twoD[0, 0] := threeD[1, 1, 1];
```

We can also use element-by-element assignment to initialize arrays. If we wanted to initialize a one-dimensional array of integers,

```
FOR i := 0 TO LEN(arr) - 1 DO
   arr[i] := 0
END
```

Or to initialize a two-dimensional array of integers,

```
FOR i := 0 TO LEN(arr, 0) - 1 DO
   FOR j := 0 TO LEN(arr, 1) - 1 DO
      arr[i, j] := 0
   END
END
```

Assigning all elements of an array at once is a bit more restrictive than element-by-element assignment. Array variables must have *exactly* the same type in order to be assigned. This means that the array length must be the same as well. For example,

```
VAR destination, source: ARRAY 100 OF INTEGER;

destination := source;
```

would assign all the elements of source to the corresponding elements of destination.

Such an assignment for a one-dimensional array has exactly the same effect as,

```
FOR i := 0 TO LEN(source) - 1 DO
    destination[i] := source[i]
END
```

Because they have the exact same type (and therefore, the exact same length), we don't need to worry about range errors.

If source and destination were two-dimensional arrays, the assignment of source to destination would be the same as,

```
FOR i := 0 TO LEN(source, 0) - 1 DO
    FOR j := 0 TO LEN(source, 1) - 1 DO
        destination[i, j] := source[i, j]
    END
END
```

String types are a special case because it is common to assign character arrays of different lengths. Hence, the predeclared procedure COPY is usually used for string assignments. As we have said before, each string should contain an 0X character as a terminator, COPY stops its operation when the 0X character is encountered. Normal array assignment is not guaranteed to stop until the full length of the array is reached.

Note: the length of the *string* is determined by the location of the terminator 0X. The string length should not be confused with LEN(s), which is the total number of array elements of s.

Some things you can keep in mind when working with assignment and arrays are the following:

To assign an entire array to another array of the *exact* same type, use normal assignment of the entire array,

```
a := b;
```

To assign arrays of different types (but with compatible elements), use element-by-element assignment,

```
FOR i := 0 TO LEN(b) - 1 DO
    a[i] := b[i]
END
```

To assign string types, use the predeclared procedure COPY,

```
COPY(source, destination);
```

12.5 Arrays as Parameters

When arrays are declared in procedure headings—that is, as parameters—size doesn't have to be specified. This is permitted so that arrays of different sizes can be passed to the procedure. This helps make procedures more **generic**—able to solve more general problems.

The **open array parameter** is a formal parameter type that is compatible with *any* array arguments that have the same dimensions and the same element type.

```
PROCEDURE ProcessTable( realTable: ARRAY OF ARRAY OF REAL);
```

The parameter `realTable` is compatible with all two-dimensional arrays that have elements of type REAL.

When declaring open parameters, ARRAY OF <type> can be declared as either a value or variable parameter. However, recall that when a value parameter is used, a copy is made of the argument.

In the example above, a copy of the argument passed to ProcessTable would be created—an entirely new array is built in computer memory. That is, space is allocated, and all the elements are copied. This can be an expensive operation in terms of memory requirements and time required to make the copy.

Because of this, array parameters are often declared as variable parameters, even though the values of the array might not change. Value parameters for arrays should be used only if there is some valid reason to do so. The type ARRAY OF CHAR is one of the few good justifications for using a value parameter of array type.

Open array parameters may have as many dimensions as your implementation permits. However, you *must* use the "long-hand" notation when writing declarations,

```
PROCEDURE DisplayMatrix( VAR i: ARRAY OF ARRAY OF INTEGER );
```

The following example shows how to use a two-dimensional array of characters. This kind of array can be thought of as a table of strings,

```
MODULE OfeMult;

(* Displays a table of strings *)

    IMPORT Out;

    CONST
        maxColumns = 27;
        maxRows = 5;

    TYPE
        StringTable = ARRAY maxRows, maxColumns OF CHAR;

    PROCEDURE Output(VAR s: ARRAY OF ARRAY OF CHAR);
    (* Does the writing of the table *)
        VAR i: INTEGER;
    BEGIN
        FOR i := 0 TO SHORT(LEN(s, 0)) - 1 DO
            Out.String(s[i]); Out.Ln
```

```
        END;
    END Output;

    PROCEDURE Do*;
    (* initializes the table and calls the procedure to write
       it out *)
        VAR str: StringTable;
    BEGIN
        str[0] := "abcdefghijklmnopqrstuvwxyz";
        str[1] := "ABCDEFGHIJKLMNOPQRSTUVWXYZ";
        str[2] := "Eric W. Nikitin";
        str[3] := "Text for the fourth row.";
        str[4] := "Fifth and last row.";
        Output(str);
    END Do;

END OfeMult.
```

Notice that when declaring the type StringTable, We could use the "short-hand" notation for declaring a two-dimensional array. But in the procedure declaration of Output, we had to use the "long-hand" notation.

In either case, the type is ARRAY OF ARRAY OF CHAR. In other words, an array of character arrays. Look at how we assigned an entire "row": str[2] := "Eric W. Nikitin". We were able to do this because the type of the row is ARRAY OF CHAR. Each dimensional "level" can be treated as a type of its own.

The following is another example:

```
TYPE
    intArray = ARRAY 10 OF INTEGER;
    intTable = ARRAY 7 OF intArray;
VAR
    iArr: intArray;
    iTab: intTable;
    ...
    iArr := iTab[0];
    (* The type of iTab[0] and iArr are both intArray. So
       the entire "row" is assigned to iArr *)
    iTab[3] := iArr;
```

12.6 Data Abstraction

One of the most important advantages to using a programming language like Oberon is its facilities for *abstraction*. We can deal with solutions to problems at a higher level without always having to think about what the computer is doing "behind the scenes." We can think in terms of information and what we want to do with that information, rather than always having to concentrate on implementation details.

Abstraction deals with information as *data structures* and a set of related operations that perform on that data.

Perhaps it would be best to provide an example. In Oberon, we talk about "strings," which are really arrays of characters. Oberon provides some built-in operations for strings. We can compare them (=, #), and we can copy one string to another. There are also facilities in modules In and Out that help us deal with strings.

For any other actions we would like to perform on strings we are forced to look at them as character arrays. There are plenty of other operations on strings that make as much sense as comparison or copying, but they aren't included in the Oberon language. So what can we do about it?

We can create a string module that contains these "missing" operations. Once we have implemented such a module, we can exclusively deal with the idea of *strings* without having to think about them as arrays of characters.

First, it is useful to know how long a string is, so let us create a Length procedure,

```
PROCEDURE Length(string: ARRAY OF CHAR): INTEGER;
(* Returns the number of characters in string *)
   VAR i: INTEGER;
BEGIN
   i := 0;
   WHILE (i < LEN(string)) & (string[i] # 0X) DO
      INC(i)
   END;
   RETURN i
END Length;
```

What else can we add to our string module? How about a way to add one string onto the end of another,

```
PROCEDURE Append*( VAR string: ARRAY OF CHAR;
                       suffix: ARRAY OF CHAR );
(* Appends 'suffix' to the end of 'string'. If there isn't
   enough room on 'string', only as much as will fit will
   be appended. 0X will be added to the end of 'string' in
   all cases *)
   VAR strLen, pos: INTEGER;
BEGIN
   strLen := Length(string);
   pos := 0;
   WHILE (pos + strLen + 1 < LEN(string)) &
         (suffix[pos] # 0X) DO
      (* stop when string runs out of room or reach the end
         of 'suffix' *)
```

```
            string[pos + strLen] := suffix[pos];
            INC(pos)
        END;
        string[pos + strLen] := 0X;
        (* make sure there is 0X as a terminator *)
    END Append;
```

Another useful operation is to search for a pattern of characters within a string,

```
PROCEDURE Find ( VAR string: ARRAY OF CHAR;
                    pattern: ARRAY OF CHAR;
                    VAR pos: LONGINT );
(*  Searches  the  first  occurrence  of  'pattern'  in
    'string'. If the pattern is found, the position of
    the first character of the pattern in 'string' is
    returned in pos. If the pattern is not found, 'pos'
    is -1. *)
    VAR   i: LONGINT;
BEGIN
    pos := -1;
    IF pattern[0] = 0X THEN RETURN END;
    (* if the pattern is an empty string, we have nothing
       to search for *)
    REPEAT
        INC(pos);
        i := 0;      (* Always start searching at the
                        beginning of the pattern *)
        WHILE  (string[i  +  pos]  =  pattern[i])  &
(pattern[i] # 0X) DO
            (* Continue as long as each character matches, and
       haven't reached the end of string or pattern *)
            INC(i)
        END; (* WHILE *)
    UNTIL (pattern[i] = 0X) OR (string[pos] = 0X);
    (* The entire pattern matched or we've reached the end
       of the string, so we're done *)
    IF (pattern[i] # 0X) THEN pos := -1 END
(* since we haven't matched, pos is set to "not found" *)

END Find;
```

Also, we might want to convert an entire string to upper-case letters,

```
PROCEDURE ToUpper(VAR in, out: ARRAY OF CHAR);
(* Copy 'in' to 'out', changing all lower-case letters to
   upper-case *)
```

```
        VAR i: INTEGER;
    BEGIN
        FOR i := 0 TO Length(in) DO
        (* for every character, including the terminating 0X *)
            IF (in[i] >= "a") & (in[i] <= "z") THEN
            (* if it's lower-case, convert to upper-case before
               assigning *)
                out[i] := CAP(in[i])
            ELSE
            (* otherwise, assign "as-is" *)
                out[i] := in[i]
            END (* IF *)
        END; (* FOR *)

    END ToUpper;
```

By now you should be getting the idea. Why should we rewrite these routines every time we need to perform them? If we write them once, and place them together in a module, we can use them over and over again. Reuse is one of the benefits of abstraction.

If our design is complete, we will have included every possible **primitive operation**—an operation that requires implementation-specific knowledge of the data structure on which it operates. In this case, any procedure that needs to know that a string is really an array of characters would be a primitive operation.

Once you have created all the primitive operations, you could continue to extend the functionality of your string module by adding other operations which are built using the primitive operations.

How do you know which operations are primitive? That is difficult to say; it is often a very subjective decision. A good deal of module design is deciding which operations are important. We certainly haven't yet defined all the primitive operations for strings, and we won't do that here. However, at this point you should begin to think of programming as defining data and the related operations *together*. This becomes very important once we start building *record types* in the next chapter.

12.7 Exercises

1. Why do you think it is necessary for Oberon to mark the end of a string with 0X? Can you think of any other way that the end of the string could be determined?

2. Explain what random access means and why it is an advantage.

3. Why do you think Oberon doesn't allow arrays (other than character arrays) to be compared? Explain possible meanings for other kinds of array comparisons.

4. Write a procedure that will initialize a four-dimensional array of reals so that all elements have a value of 0.0. Use open array parameters.

5. Write a procedure that takes an integer array of any size and sorts the numbers in ascending order.

6. Write a procedure that takes an array of strings and sorts them in descending order.

7. Write a procedure that is passed a date in the format 'YYYYMMDD', and converts it to other formats specified by a "format string" that uses the symbols 'Y' for year, 'M' for month, and 'D' for day. For example,

```
ToDate("19970203", "MM-DD-YY", destination);
```

8. Write the following procedures to add to the Strings module presented in this chapter,

   a) Index—search for the first occurrence of a character in a string
   b) Substr—extract a "sub-string" from a string based on position and length of the portion to be extracted.
   c) Reverse—reverse a string in place.
   d) Insert—insert one string into another based on position in the target string.
   e) ToLower—convert a string to all lowercase (in place).

9. Write a function GCD(x, y) using Euclid's algorithm for greatest common divisor. x and y are integers and the function returns an integer. The inner loop is as follows:

```
WHILE y > 0 DO
   r := x MOD y;
   x := y;
   y := r
END; (* WHILE *)
```

10. Write your own version of the standard procedure COPY.

Chapter 13
Record Types

13.1 Declaring Record Types

Records are a way of packaging related information together. Records are invaluable for creating abstractions. We can group information together, rather than just treat data as a series of unrelated numbers and letters.

```
MODULE OfeRecord;

(* Demonstrates declaration of a record type, and use of
   record variables *)

   IMPORT Out;

   TYPE
      Car = RECORD
      (* declaring a new type 'Car' to be a record type *)
         year: INTEGER;
         make: ARRAY 12 OF CHAR;
         price: REAL
      END; (* Car has three fields: year, make, and price *)

   PROCEDURE Execute*;
   (* Define two variables of record type, and initialize
      them both *)
      VAR carA, carB: Car;
      (* Both a and b have type 'Car' *)
   BEGIN
      carA.year := 1996;        (* initialize carA *)
      carA.make := "Ford";
      carA.price := 25450.99;

      carB := carA;             (* initialize carB *)
```

```
    Out.Int(carB.year, 0); Out.Ln;
    Out.String(carB.make); Out.Ln;
    Out.Real(carB.price, 9); Out.Ln
  END Execute;
```

```
END OfeRecord.
```

Declaring a record type is done in a manner similar to how we declared a type in the last chapter. But with a record type, you need to include the keyword RECORD after the type name and '=':

```
Car = RECORD
```

This tells the compiler we want to declare `Car` to be a record type. Next we need to describe the information the record is to hold,

```
year: INTEGER;
make: ARRAY 12 OF CHAR;
price: REAL
```

Any variable defined to be of type `Car` can hold these three pieces of information *all at the same time*. After we have declared the record type, we can define variables of that type,

```
VAR carA, carB: Car;
```

Variables carA and carB have been allocated with enough space so that each one can hold an integer value, an array of character values, and a real value. Since each carA and carB has information that belongs exclusively to itself, we need to be able to associate carA and carB with their *data fields*,

```
carA.year := 1996;
```

The "dot notation" is used to access each field of a record variable. The designator 'carA.year' refers to a specific data field associated with carA. We declared 'year' as type INTEGER, so 'carA.year' can be used just like any other integer variable. Hence, we can assign the value '1996' to it. We can do the same thing to the other fields of carA,

```
carA.make := "Ford";
carA.price := 25450.99;
```

Now remember records were described as a way to "package" data. An advantage of that packaging is being able to deal with the entire record at once, as we did here,

```
carB := carA;
```

This assigns *each field of carA to the corresponding field of carB*. It has the same effect as if we had assigned each field individually. The rest of procedure Execute should be easy to figure out, so let us continue on to talk more about records.

13.2 Details of Record Types

Records are *structured types*, like arrays. But unlike arrays, the elements don't have to all be the same type. Records are **heterogeneous**—made up of different kinds of values. Elements within a record are called **fields**. Each field is named (given an identifier) and given a type.

Records model rows in a table. Each row in the table is a single record. For example,

	year	make	price
carA =>	1996	"Ford"	25450.99
carB =>	1996	"Ford"	25450.99

Records make it possible to refer either to the entire collection of data or to individual elements.

Record types are declared by giving a name to the record type as a whole, then providing a list of record fields. The field list looks very much like a list of variable definitions, and it must appear between the reserved words RECORD and END.

The fields can be of *any* basic or structured type. So a record field can be another record—or it can be an array. Also, an array may have records as its elements. So by using structured types, we can build some very complex and useful structures from a few simple pieces.

There is a restriction, however; a record type may not have a field whose type is the record itself. That is, *recursive type declarations* are illegal,

```
TYPE
   ThisType = RECORD
      a: INTEGER;
      b: ThisType        (* Error! You can't define a
                           record type within itself! *)
   END;
```

An advantage of record types is that related information can be grouped together and dealt with as a single unit, rather than separate parts. The following is a mathematical example that could also be used as a starting place for a simple, two-dimensional (2D) drawing program. A point can be used as the basic building block on a plane, and is defined by x and y coordinates,

```
TYPE
   Point = RECORD
      x: REAL;
      y: REAL
   END;
```

Just as is done in variable definitions, we could instead declare x and y as a comma-separated list because they have the same type,

```
TYPE
    Point = RECORD              (* this is equivalent to the
                                previous Point declaration *)
        x, y: REAL
    END;
```

Point can now be used just like any built-in type. For instance, we could define a variable of type Point,

```
VAR
    p: Point;
```

Also, since Point is now officially recognized as a type, we can use it to build other types. For example, a circle is defined by a center point and a radius,

```
TYPE
    Circle = RECORD
        center: Point;          (* center is a Point, it has
                                fields x and y *)
        radius: REAL
    END;

VAR
    c: Circle;
```

How do we access the information in the record variable? That is, how do we assign values to fields, or otherwise get information out of fields?

Oberon uses the "dot notation" to access individual fields. They are accessed by using the record variable name followed by a ' . ' and then the field name,

```
p.x := 4.0;
p.y := 6.5;
c.radius := 2.25;
```

Since the field center in a Circle is of type Point, you need to have another dot "level" to get to center's fields,

```
c.center.x := 3.3;
c.center.y := 5.6;
```

We have seen that you can assign values to a record's fields one at a time using the dot notation. Is there a way to assign entire records? Similar to other types in Oberon, records of the same type can be assigned to one another. Since center and p are of the same record type (i.e., Point),

```
c.center := p;
```

which has the exact same effect as,

```
c.center.x := p.x;
c.center.y := p.y;
```

That is, each field is assigned to the corresponding field of the target.

Record variables can be treated as "whole entities" when being assigned to one another. However, they can't be operands in other types of expressions, nor can they be compared to one another.

```
IF  c.center  #  p  THEN  ...  (*  Error!  Can't  compare
                                    record variables *)

circ.center := c.center + p;    (* Error! Can't add
                                    record variables *)
```

Just like array variables, a variable of record type can be declared anonymously,

```
VAR
    p: Point;
    q: RECORD x, y: REAL END;

    (* 'q' has the same structure as 'p'; but they are
        different types *)

    . . .
    q := p;  (* Error! 'p' and 'q' are different types! *)
```

The general form of a record type declaration is

```
TYPE
    <type name> = RECORD
        <field list>
    END;
```

13.3 Records and Arrays

Suppose we wanted to create a database for a collection of books. Each book has a title, author, library of Congress number, and a short description. We might declare a book type as,

```
TYPE
    Book = RECORD
        title, author, locNum: ARRAY 64 OF CHAR;
        desc: ARRAY 256 OF CHAR;
    END;
```

We could define a variable of type Book,

```
VAR
    thisBook: Book;
```

To initialize thisBook we could write

```
thisBook.title := "Oberon-2 Programming";
thisBook.author := "Eric W. Nikitin";
thisBook.locNum := "QA76.1234.N456 1997";
thisBook.desc := "A great programming book for Oberon-2";
```

But because a database would have to deal with multiple books, we might want to define an entire array of Books,

```
VAR
    library: ARRAY 1000 OF Book;
```

How can we access fields in such an array of records? Arrays require an index to locate the element we want to access. So, we use square brackets and an integer index, just like the arrays we have seen already. But we have to add the dot notation to get to the fields for each element,

```
library[0].title := "Oberon-2 Programming";
library[0].author := "Eric W. Nikitin";
library[0].locNum := "QA76.1234.N456 1997";
library[0].desc := "A great programming book for Oberon-2";
```

The variable library is the array, so the bracketed index is associated with library.

```
library.title[0] := "Oberon-2 Programming";(* ERROR!!! *)
```

This would be wrong because library is an array—not a record.

Also notice that the fields of Book are arrays. So we could write

```
library[0].title[0] := "O";
```

The field title is an ARRAY OF CHAR. So library[0].title[0] is valid and means assign the letter "O" to the 0th element of title (ARRAY OF CHAR) in the 0th element of library (ARRAY OF Book).

The dot notation combined with array brackets may take some getting used to, but it is actually very straightforward.

```
library[1] := thisBook;
```

would assign each field of thisBook to the corresponding field of library[1]. That is, the above assignment is equivalent to

```
library[1].title := thisBook.title;
library[1].author := thisBook.author;
library[1].locNum := thisBook.locNum;
library[1].desc := thisBook.desc;
```

Remember that record-to-record assignments are allowed only with records of the same type. thisBook and library[1] have the same type (i.e., Book).

Also remember that even though we can perform assignments of whole records, we cannot do comparisons (=, >, <, #, etc.) of record variables. Records must be compared on a field by field basis.

13.4   Exporting Record Types

As with the other language structures we have discussed, types can also be exported. Add the export mark '*' after the name of the type, and that type is then usable in any importing module. For a simple declared type,

```
TYPE
    String* = ARRAY 256 OF CHAR;
```

With record types it is only slightly more complicated. Since each field is named, we must specify an export mark by each field that is to be exported. Fields that aren't exported are still there, but they are *hidden* from external view. They can be accessed only by procedures within the module where they were declared. You don't see them in the module's definition and you can't assign to them or see them from outside the module.

Exported fields are also called **public fields**. Unmarked fields are also known as **private fields**, because they are "private" to the module where the record type is declared.

```
TYPE
    Book* = RECORD
        title*, author*, locNum*: ARRAY 64 OF CHAR;
        desc*: ARRAY 256 OF CHAR;
        sequence: LONGINT;
    END;
```

The fields title, author, locNum, and desc would be visible in importing modules. The sequence field is not exported and is therefore hidden. Note that you can export a type without exporting *any* of its fields, completely hiding all of them.

But you must export the type itself in order to export its fields. In order to export title, you *must* first export Book.

Why would we want to hide record fields? The answer has to do with concepts of data abstraction and *encapsulation*. Recall that when designing modules, we strive to define a set of operations for a particular type of data. This helps make things simpler, and keeps the module at a more understandable level. By hiding implementation details and allowing the user of the module to see only the "important" things, we don't have to look at the whole problem at once. We can break it into parts we can more easily understand.

The module and export structures of Oberon allow us to separate the interface from the implementation. When we use a module—we need to see only the *essential* parts of that module.

We can thus "layer" our programs, and also create libraries of types and procedures that we can use over and over. We don't have to "start from scratch" each time we need a particular set of functionality. In the next chapter, we will see another way of "layering" our programs.

Once a record field is hidden, it can be accessed only by procedures defined within the module where it is declared. So Oberon defines two kinds of export marks: the '*' we have seen already, and the '-', which is known as a **read-only** mark. By making a global variable or record field read-only, we can control how and when the values are changed, and yet look at the value at any time.

Internal procedures are still required to modify read-only fields and variables, but external modules can examine the value. The read-only export mark may appear wherever an export mark is allowed.

Module In has a global variable that should, in fact, have been defined as read-only,

```
VAR Done-: BOOLEAN;
```

In.Done should never be changed outside of module In. In.Done tells us whether the input procedures have worked correctly and so should be set only within those procedures. A user of module In only needs to check the value of In.Done, and never has a reason to change it.

13.5 Exercises

1. Describe record types and how they are useful. Explain what fields are, as well.

2. Why do you think that a record type cannot contain a field that is its own type? That is, why are recursive type declarations illegal?

3. Declare a Square type and a Rectangle type (you may use the Point type declared in this chapter). What information is needed to describe squares and rectangles?

4. Declare an array type that has Squares as elements. Write a procedure to initialize your array (what are logical initial values?).

5. Declare a Fraction type. Write the following procedures that operate on your Fraction type:

    a. a function that converts a fraction's value to a decimal number.
    b. InFrac and OutFrac to read in and write out fractions written in the form a/b.
    c. a boolean function IsProper()
    d. a function that returns the sum of two fractions.
    e. a function that returns a fraction in lowest terms. (*Hint*: You can use the GCD() function from the last chapter.)
    f. functions to subtract, multiply, and divide fractions.

6. Declare a Card type which models playing cards (how would you represent suits and the card value?). If you wanted to design a computer card game, how would you simulate shuffling the deck? How can you guarantee that the deck will be shuffled differently each time? (*Hint*: Can you think of a way to generate "random" numbers?)

7. Write procedures to shuffle a deck of 52 cards, and deal out hands to up to four players. (*Hint*: Is there a library module available with your compiler that provides a random number generator?)

Chapter 14
Extending Record Types

14.1 Type Extension of Records

Type extension provides us with another way to "layer" modules. Type extension allows the programmer to extend an existing record type by adding new fields. In Oberon, the "new" *extended type* is still compatible with the "old" *base type*.

Examine the following set of three related modules:

```
MODULE OfeCars;

(* Declare a type 'Car' and procedures that act on it *)

   TYPE
      Car* = RECORD
         year-: INTEGER;
         make-: ARRAY 12 OF CHAR;
         price-: REAL
      END;

   PROCEDURE Init*(VAR c: Car;
                       year: INTEGER;
                       make: ARRAY OF CHAR;
                       price: REAL);
   (* Used to initialize variables of type Car *)
   BEGIN
      c.year := year;
      COPY(make, c.make);
      c.price := price
   END Init;

END OfeCars.
```

```
MODULE OfeLuxury;

(*  Declare  a  type  'LuxuryCar'  which  is  extended  from
    'OfeCars.Car' *)

   IMPORT OfeCars;

   TYPE
      LuxuryCar* = RECORD (OfeCars.Car)
         packageCode-: INTEGER
      END;

   PROCEDURE Init*(VAR l: LuxuryCar;
                   year: INTEGER;
                   make: ARRAY OF CHAR;
                   price: REAL;
                   packCode: INTEGER);
   (* Used to initialize variables of type LuxuryCar *)
   BEGIN
      OfeCars.Init(l, year, make, price);
      l.packageCode := packCode
   END Init;

END OfeLuxury.

MODULE OfeTestcar;

(* Used to test module OfeLuxury *)

   IMPORT OfeLuxury, Out;

   PROCEDURE Test*;
   (* Initialize a LuxuryCar variable and display the values
      *)
      VAR car1: OfeLuxury.LuxuryCar;
   BEGIN
      OfeLuxury.Init(car1, 1996, "Lexus", 35000.0, 13);
      Out.Int(car1.year, 0); Out.Ln;
      Out.String(car1.make); Out.Ln;
      Out.Real(car1.price, 0); Out.Ln;
      Out.Int(car1.packageCode, 0); Out.Ln
   END Test;

END OfeTestcar.
```

First, let us look at the module OfeCars. It declares a record type `Car`, which is just like the example in the previous chapter,

```
Car* = RECORD
    year-: INTEGER;
    make-: ARRAY 12 OF CHAR;
    price-: REAL
END;
```

The only difference is that we have added export marks. Notice the read-only marks used in the record fields. We have also declared a procedure Init. Because Car's fields are all read-only, we *must* define procedures to modify them. This is consistent with the idea of abstraction that we already discussed. Car is an *abstract data type*, and Init is its sole operation.

We could add additional operations, but for demonstration purposes we will keep things simple. Next, module OfeLuxury imports OfeCars, and we declare another type,

```
LuxuryCar* = RECORD (OfeCars.Car)
    packageCode-: INTEGER
END;
```

Notice the qualified identifier `OfeCars.Car` in parentheses after the word RECORD. By declaring LuxuryCar in this manner, we have made LuxuryCar an *extension* of Car. Car is the *base type*, and LuxuryCar is the *extended type*. LuxuryCar has all of the fields declared in Car, *and* declares a new field of its own, `packageCode`.

Because we want LuxuryCar to be an abstract data type, we declare procedure Init. Notice that we call OfeCars.Init from within OfeLuxury.Init. This is done for two reasons. First, we want to reuse as much of what we have written before as we can. Also, the fields of Car are declared as read-only; because LuxuryCar is declared in another module, we cannot directly modify Car's fields, even though LuxuryCar is an extension to Car.

Let us point out something that might seem strange in OfeLuxury.Init,

```
OfeCars.Init(l, year, make, price);
```

How can we call OfeCars.Init with `l` as its first argument? The `l` parameter has type LuxuryCar—doesn't the argument have to be a Car variable? Under certain circumstances, Oberon allows extended types to be used in place of the base type. In a manner of speaking, LuxuryCar *is* a type of Car—or to be more precise, LuxuryCar is a *subtype* of Car.

Module OfeTestcar should be fairly straightforward; so let us continue on to talk more about extended types.

14.2 Details of Extended Record Types

Type extension is one of the main features that was added to the Oberon language when it was created as a successor to Modula-2. Type extension—sometimes called *record extension*—applies *only* to record types. That is, only record types may be extended.

How do you create an extended type? You take an existing type—a record type that exists in a library, or one that you've declared yourself—and extend it by adding new fields to it. This is helpful as a means of reuse; to build on existing types, and a way to logically group and structure parts of our programs into types and subtypes.

The general form of an extended record type is

```
TYPE
    <extended type> = RECORD (<base type>)
        <new fields>
    END;
```

In the declaration of the extended type, the base type appears in parentheses after the keyword RECORD. The extended type adds new fields to those of the base type—it has all the fields of the base, as well as those it added. The extended type can be regarded as a *specialization* of its base type.

Extensions are usually declared in a module different from the base type. In this case, the base type must be a qualified identifier; and as always, only the exported fields of the base type are visible to the extension. If there is some need for the extended type to have access to the private fields of the base type, then the extension *must be declared within the same module as the base.*

All the fields of an extended record variable are referenced in the usual manner using the dot notation.

As a further example, let us extend the Point type we declared earlier. Recall that Point is declared as

```
Point = RECORD
    x, y: REAL
END;
```

Now suppose we wanted to create a three-dimensional (3D) Point type. We could declare it as

```
Point3D = RECORD
    x, y, z: REAL
END;
```

But that provides no relationship between a 3D point and a regular (2D) point. In Oberon, such a relationship can be created:

```
Point3D = RECORD (Point)
    z: REAL
END;
```

We can define variables using either declaration of Point3D, and in most ways, they would behave in an identical manner,

```
VAR
    p3D: Point3D;
BEGIN
    p3D.x := 1.0;
    p3D.y := 2.0;
    p3D.z := 3.0;
```

These assignments work equally well for either declaration of Point3D. However, there is one significant difference in the second declaration of Point3D—it is a subtype of Point. There is an explicit base-extension relationship between the two.

Oberon provides a way to "map" extended types back into their base types. Recall that when making assignments between record variables of identical type, assignment is equivalent to assigning each field individually. When an extended variable is assigned to a variable of the base type, only those fields declared in the base type are assigned. For example,

```
VAR
    p: Point; p3D: Point3D;
BEGIN
    ...
    p := p3D;
```

What exactly happens in this assignment? Basically, p3D is treated as a Point. That is, we assign the fields that p3D "inherited" from the base type Point. Therefore the assignment, p := p3D; would be equivalent to

```
p.x := p3D.x;
p.y := p3D.y;
```

What about p3D.z? Point p doesn't have a z field, so that information isn't assigned—it's lost in the "mapping."

Can we assign a Point to a Point3D? Because p doesn't have all the information necessary to completely "fill-in" p3D, we can't directly assign p to p3D. Therefore, assigning a variable of the base type to one of the extended type is *illegal* in Oberon.

```
p3D := p;    (* ERROR! Illegal assignment *)
```

There simply isn't enough information to complete the assignment. If you wanted to transfer Point information into a Point3D, you'd have to assign the fields one at a time.

This is a very important point to remember—in Oberon, an extended type is compatible with its base type.

14.3 Subtyping

As has been said, type extension sets up an explicit relationship between base and extended types. This is called a subtype relationship. Subtyping expresses a "kind of" relationship between base and extension. That is, each extension is a "kind of" the base type. For instance,

```
TYPE
    Fruit = RECORD ...
    END;

    Apple = RECORD (Fruit) ...
    END;

    Orange = RECORD (Fruit) ...
    END;

    McIntosh = RECORD (Apple) ...
    END;

    GrannySmith = RECORD (Apple) ...
    END;
```

The original base type is Fruit. The others have all been defined as types of Fruit. Apple and Orange are *direct extensions* of Fruit—they have been declared with Fruit as their *direct base type*. McIntosh and GrannySmith have been extended from Apple. But they are not only types of Apple, but are also indirectly types of Fruit. Whatever fields were defined in Fruit also exist in McIntosh and GrannySmith.

Setting up subtype relationships gives several advantages.

We can declare operations (procedures) for dealing with Fruit, and those operations may also be applicable to Fruit's sub-types.

The subtype relationship also helps in program design. We can express logical relationships, which form a hierarchy. For example,

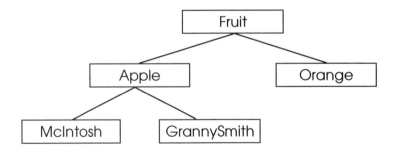

The subtype relationship is also referred to as inheritance—the subtype "inherits" attributes from the base type. Type extension provides **data inheritance**—data fields are inherited by subtypes.

Subtyping contributes greatly to the notion of data abstraction. This is a building block for *object-oriented programming*. When we discuss *type-bound procedures*, we will see how to not only inherit data fields—but also inheritance of operations (procedures). The ability to inherit procedures can be thought of as **functional inheritance**—inheriting the functionality of a type.

14.4 Records as Parameters

As with any type in Oberon, records can be used as parameters in procedure declarations. Recall that when making a procedure call, the type of the argument must be compatible with the type of the actual parameter.

As we have seen before, a value parameter produces a copy of the argument. Arguments of record types work in exactly the same manner. For example, if we declare

```
PROCEDURE Display(p: Point);
BEGIN
   Out.Int(p.x, 0); Out.Ln;
   Out.Int(p.y, 0); Out.Ln
END Display;
```

and make a call to Display,

```
Display(q);
```

a copy of the record q is made. During the procedure call, p is allocated as a Point type. The values of q's fields are copied to p's fields,

q.x is copied to p.x
q.y is copied to p.y

As long as the actual type of q is compatible with Point, then there is no problem in making the copy. This means that the actual type of q *must* be either Point or a subtype of Point.

```
VAR q: Point3D;
...
Display(q);    (* legal procedure call - Point3D is a
                  subtype of Point *)
```

Variable parameters follow the same compatibility rule. But because a variable parameter is a reference to the argument, no copying is performed. So if Display was instead declared as,

```
PROCEDURE Display(VAR p: POINT);
```

in the call Display(q), p *refers to* q. The *actual type* of p during the call remains Point3D. But because Point3D is extended from Point, p can be treated as though it were really a Point. Variables of type Point3D have all the attributes of Point; any extra information it contains can be safely ignored.

As with arrays, records are very often declared as variable parameters for efficiency reasons, even if they remain unchanged by the procedure.

14.5   Abstraction and Encapsulation

We have talked about the notion of abstraction and how it applies to program design. *Encapsulation* is another concept that we have touched on, but haven't yet discussed in detail. **Encapsulation** is the hiding of specific details of an implementation; only the interface is visible. Encapsulation is also known as *information hiding*.

Oberon promotes encapsulation through its module structure, the use of export marks, and the import statement. This is different from many other programming languages, in which there is no separate language construct for encapsulation; types (usually referred to as *classes* in these languages) provide the mechanism for both abstraction and encapsulation.

In Oberon, however, types support abstraction whereas modules support encapsulation. This means that several related types can be implemented in the same module. In that case, the types have access to each other's implementations, which is sometimes a requirement.

Keep in mind that if an extension is declared in a module separate from its base, it has no access to the base's implementation. If types and subtypes are designed carefully, this shouldn't be a drawback—all of the base's primitive operations would already be defined. Any extensions could be built from those primitives.

Abstraction and encapsulation are complimentary concepts—they work best when considered together. Their use implies greater responsibility on the programmer's part. The source text of a module may not be available; users of such a module have knowledge only of the module's interface.

We should therefore make great attempts at keeping modules readable—with meaningful type and procedure names. Documentation, in the form of exported comments, can also be very important. If such comments aren't sufficient, then external documentation on the use of a module should be provided as well.

Extension layers should also be kept as *shallow* as possible. It is more difficult to understand a type if attributes are located in some distant, indirect base type. Multiple layers are also a potential source of run-time inefficiency. Be sure that, as you extend types, the extensions are logical and consistent.

Software quality is dependent on a program having the following attributes:

- Correct—it operates as intended.
- Robust—it can deal with any reasonably anticipated problems.
- Portable—it can be moved to another compiler with few changes.
- Efficient.
- Easy to use.

None of these things will happen by accident. We must design from the start with the intention of producing programs with these qualities. Proper use of abstraction and encapsulation are a great help in producing quality software.

14.6 Exercises

1. Describe the relationships between base types and extended types.

2. Explain the advantages of specifying subtype relationships.

3. Consider the following modules:

```
MODULE M;

    TYPE T* = RECORD
             a: INTEGER
        END;

END M.

MODULE N;

    IMPORT M;

    TYPE U* = RECORD (M.T)
             b*: REAL
        END;

END N.

MODULE P;

    IMPORT N;

    TYPE V* = RECORD (N.U)
             a*: LONGINT
        END;

END P.
```

Is the declaration of V in module P valid? What if M were changed so that the field a from M.T were exported? Explain your reasoning.

4. Declare a type Employee that holds an employee's name, a salary, and a date of hire. Then declare a type Supervisor that has all the attributes of Employee, but in addition, has a list of up to 10 employees and an assistant who work for the supervisor. Write procedures to initialize both Employee and Supervisor, and to set values for fields (raiseSalary, for instance).

5. What would happen if you wanted to use the types from exercise 4 to create a database for an entire organization? How would you handle multiple levels (i.e., a supervisor is also an employee and might have her own supervisor, who in turn would have a supervisor... all the way up to the president of the company)? Is there anything you should be careful about? Is there anything you would change from the way you designed the types previously?

Chapter 15
Pointer Types

15.1   What Are Pointers?

The concept of a pointer is, in essence, a very simple notion. However, pointers are often a great source of confusion for novice programmers. So, unlike other chapters, we will start off here with a discussion before seeing an example.

Let us review arrays for a moment. Arrays are very useful structures, but they have some limitations:

- They have fixed size, limiting the number of elements that can be inserted.
- They can be difficult to reorder. In arrays, logical and physical order are *bound together*. If you want to sort an array, you must physically move elements around.
- Insertion and deletion of elements can be difficult.

However, pointers can be used to create **dynamic data structures**—structures that grow and shrink during runtime. Dynamic data structures can get around the limitations of arrays.

A **pointer** refers to a location—it represents a computer memory address. We can think of computer memory as a huge array where the position in the array is the location's *address*.

A pointer is analogous to an index into that huge memory array. The pointer shows the *location* of the value we wish to access. A pointer's *actual value*—which we can never really see—is a memory address. A pointer "points" to a memory location.

<= computer memory =>

The location stores a value. The pointer shows us where the location is.

We can use an analogy of an extremely long row of mailboxes. Each mailbox has an address. The mailbox can hold a value—the pointer shows us which mailbox to look at.

Now, how do we make use of pointers in Oberon? Recall that when we define variables, computer memory is allocated for us; the Oberon compiler decides how much memory to allocate. We don't need to worry about *where* it is allocated—that is done automatically. When we define program variables, we are in effect *grabbing pieces of memory*.

Pointers, on the other hand, let us *dynamically* allocate record and array variables. That is, we can create a record or array as we need it. Let us look at an example:

```
MODULE OfePoint;

(* To demonstrate the use of pointers *)

    IMPORT Out;

    TYPE
        CarPtr* = POINTER TO CarRec;        (* Here is the
                                               pointer type
                                               declaration *)
        CarRec* = RECORD        (* And the record type being
                                   pointed to *)
            year: INTEGER;
            make: ARRAY 12 OF CHAR;
            price: REAL
        END;

    PROCEDURE Init*(c: CarPtr; year: INTEGER; make: ARRAY OF
                    CHAR; price: REAL);
    (* Initializes a record pointed to by c. Do you notice
       anything unusual about the declaration c: CarPtr? *)
    BEGIN
        c.year := year;
        COPY(make, c.make);
        c.price := price
    END Init;

    PROCEDURE Display*(c: CarPtr);
    (* Displays the values in the record pointed to by c *)
    BEGIN
        Out.Int(c.year, 0); Out.Ln;
        Out.String(c.make); Out.Ln;
        Out.Real(c.price, 0); Out.Ln
    END Display;
```

```
PROCEDURE Test*;

(* Allocates a CarRec, initializes it, and then displays
   the values *)
   VAR car: CarPtr;
BEGIN
   NEW(car);
   Init(car, 1994, "Toyota", 26000.00);
   Display(car);
END Test;
```

```
END OfePoint.
```

OfePoint *could* have been written without using pointers; in this example, there is no unique problem that requires the use of pointers. We could have just used an ordinary record. But because pointers can cause some confusion, it is best to keep things on somewhat familiar ground for the first example.

The first new thing we encounter in OfePoint is the pointer type declaration,

```
CarPtr* = POINTER TO CarRec;
```

which shouldn't be too difficult to understand. The type CarPtr is declared as a pointer to a record type—in this case, CarRec. The only unusual thing to note is that CarRec itself hasn't been declared at that point in the program. Pointer types are allowed to be declared in this way; the record or array type being pointed to *must* be declared eventually, but the pointer declaration can come first. (This is another kind of forward declaration.)

CarRec is almost exactly like the type OfeCars.Car, except the fields of CarRec are hidden by not exporting them. If we were to import OfePoint into another module, we would have to use procedures like Init and Display to access the fields of CarRec.

Procedures Init and Display should seem straightforward, except perhaps for one thing: Init changes the values of the fields c.year, c.make, and c.price, and yet c is declared as a *value parameter*. The reason this is possible is because a pointer, like a variable parameter, makes a *reference to a variable*. The pointer itself cannot be changed, but the variable it points to can be changed. Now,

```
VAR car: CarPtr;
```

defines a pointer variable of type CarPtr. We intended for car to point at a CarRec, but at this stage in the program, that isn't the case. The variable car points to *nothing*—we haven't told it what we want it to point to. We need to initialize it first—to set it to point to something.

Where do we get a record variable of type CarRec that we can point to? The predeclared procedure NEW can be used to allocate a record variable. The statement,

```
NEW(car);
```

does two things: it allocates a record variable of the correct type, in this case a CarRec; and it then sets car to point to that record variable. NEW *knows* to allocate a CarRec because of the declaration of CarPtr—`car` is allowed to point to variables only of type CarRec. The call to Init is then required to initialize the fields of the record pointed to by `car`.

Up to now, we have been able to use variables to *directly* access values. But with pointers, we have introduced a "middle-man"; pointers are used to *indirectly* access values. That is why the term *indirection* is often used when discussing pointer operations.

If you are a bit confused right now, don't feel bad. Pointers are a common source of confusion. Take your time with this concept—it is an important and powerful one. Get used to the idea of indirectly operating on values. It is absolutely essential to understand the difference between pointers and the locations they address.

15.2   Details of Pointers

Pointers allow us to perform **dynamic allocation**—to create records and arrays as needed at run-time. This section will concentrate on describing pointers to records, although much of what is discussed applies to pointers to arrays as well.

The definition of a pointer variable doesn't produce the record variable it points to. The record must be explicitly created using the predeclared procedure NEW. The argument to NEW must be a pointer type. Recall that a pointer type is declared to point to a specific type of record; a pointer variable can point only to that type of record. So even though the argument to NEW is a pointer, it is obvious what type of record to allocate.

When a record is allocated by NEW, the record itself is **anonymous**—it doesn't have a name of its own (unlike when we define an ordinary record variable). The pointer then gets the address that marks the location of that record. The record cannot be accessed directly, but only through the pointer.

```
VAR car: CarPtr;
...
NEW(car);(* a CarRec is allocated, and car points to
          it *)
```

There are very few operations permitted on pointer variables. They may be assigned to other pointer variables of compatible type, or compared for equality or inequality.

Pointers can be assigned the predefined value NIL. The value NIL is a "non-location"; that is, it points to nothing. A pointer that equals NIL doesn't address a location. NIL is a special value in that it is compatible with any pointer type,

```
car := NIL;    (* car is initialized to NIL (car
               points to nothing) *)
```

Many implementations initialize pointer variables to NIL for safety reasons. This is not guaranteed, so be sure to initialize pointer variables before using them.

Ordinary variables name a piece of memory. An assignment to an ordinary variable *changes the value stored there.* Making an assignment to a pointer variable does the same thing, only, as we have seen, the value of the pointer variable *is* an address.

The assignment to a pointer *changes the location it represents.* When a pointer is assigned the value of another pointer, they both address the same location. The assignment does *not* change the values that are stored at that location,

```
VAR car1, car2: CarPtr;
...
NEW(car1);
car2 := car1;(* car1 and car2 now point to the same
                 record; the record itself has not
                 been changed *)
```

The terms "location," "anonymous variable," and "value addressed by a pointer" all mean exactly the same thing.

Can we use pointers to change the values in the records they point to? Assigning *through* a pointer changes the values stored at the location. Changing the values of the fields of the anonymous record can be accomplished as either field-by-field assignment, or all at once by *dereferencing* the record with the '^' operator. (Recall that, on some Oberon systems, the '^' is represented as an upward pointing arrow '↑'.)

Field-by-field assignment can be done in exactly the same way as with fields of ordinary record variables by using the dot notation,

```
car1.year := 1995;
car1.make := car2.make;
car1.price := car2.price * 0.75;
```

The value of the pointer car1 stays the same; it still points to the same record. However, the values of the record's fields have been changed.

We can also perform assignments of entire records. As with normal records, they must both have the same type (or extended types can be assigned to base types). We cannot do the assignment *directly*—direct assignment changes the value of the pointer, not the record. We need to *dereference* the pointer using the '^' operator,

```
NEW(car2);(* If car2 doesn't point to a record, we
              need to allocate one *)

car2^ := car1^;(* All the fields of the record pointed
                   to by car1 are assigned to the
                   fields of the record pointed to by
                   car2 *)
```

The **dereference operator** '^' can also be used to access individual fields. However, its use is optional when dereferencing fields,

```
car2^.year := car1^.year; (* The same as car2.year :=
                              car1.year *)
```

Dereferenced pointer variables can be assigned to and from ordinary records as well,

```
VAR ptr: CarPtr; rec: CarRec;
...        (* Assume that rec is initialized here *)
NEW(ptr);
ptr := car;(* ERROR! Assignment of record to pointer *)
ptr^ := car; (* OK. Assignment of record to record *)
```

NIL pointers cannot be dereferenced. They don't point to valid record variables, and attempts to access them will result in a trap at run-time,

```
car1 := NIL;

car2.year := car1.year; (* ERROR! car1 is NIL which
                            causes a trap. *)

car2^ := car1^;  (* ERROR! car1 is NIL which causes a
                     trap. *)
```

Comparisons of pointer variables are performed using the '=' and '#' operators. These operators are used to test whether two pointers have the same value; that is, to check if they point to the same location. Be careful you don't confuse the "equality" of pointers with "equality" of the values contained in the locations they point to.

NIL may be used in comparisons to every type of pointer,

```
IF car1 = car2 THEN ... (* TRUE if car1 and car2 point
                            to the same record, or
                            they're both NIL *)
IF car1 = NIL THEN ...   (* TRUE if car1 has a value
                            of NIL *)
IF car1 # NIL THEN ...   (* TRUE if car1 is not
                            equal to NIL *)
```

Dereferenced pointers cannot be compared directly, just like ordinary record variables. If dereferenced fields are basic types, then they can, of course, be compared,

```
IF car1^ = car2^ THEN ...
(* ERROR! You can't compare records! *)

IF car1.year = car2.year THEN ...
(* OK. INTEGER comparison; assuming neither car1 nor
    car2 is NIL *)
```

The general form of a pointer declaration is,

```
TYPE
   <identifier> = POINTER TO <record or array type>;
```

Similar to array and record variable definitions, pointer variables may be declared of anonymous pointer type,

```
VAR  ptr: POINTER TO CarRec;
     ptrToRec: POINTER TO RECORD x, y: INTEGER END;
```

15.3 Memory Management and Pointers

For Oberon, most management of computer memory resources is controlled automatically by the run-time environment. Let us look briefly at how this is done.

Allocation of computer memory for a module—including memory for its procedures, global variables, and for any statements that appear in the module's body—is performed (at the latest) when any exported identifier is first used. That is, if the module is not already loaded into memory, it will be loaded as soon as it is used. These resources are *statically* allocated, which means they exist in memory as long as the module remains loaded.

During procedure call, any memory needed for the procedure's local variables (including parameters) is allocated at the time of the call. This memory is tied up only as long as the procedure is active; it is automatically freed when the procedure ends. Because procedures call other procedures, there needs to be a way to keep track of all of these procedure invocations. The management of this memory is envisioned as a *stack*—we talked briefly about the stack when discussing traps. The amount of memory used by the stack changes as procedures are called—it shrinks and grows. The memory allocation for the stack is *dynamic*.

Pointer variables themselves are allocated either globally (for global pointer variables), or on the stack (for local variables). However, allocation of records and arrays by procedure NEW can occur at any time. So it makes sense to manage these types of objects in their own special place in memory. Records and arrays allocated via NEW are usually kept in a place in memory called the *heap*. Heap allocation is also dynamic.

The management of the heap could present a particular problem—if left unchecked it would continue to grow every time NEW was called. Eventually, you'd run out of memory. Some languages require programmers to free heap-allocated memory themselves—via procedures with names such as FREE, DISPOSE, or DEALLOCATE.

This manual memory management is another source of concern, and is often very error prone. For example, suppose an anonymous record is freed, but pointers still point to it; accessing such a record could easily cause a program crash.

Or suppose there are no longer any pointers that point to a particular anonymous record. Those records can no longer be accessed at all; that memory is considered still in use, but there is no way to free it. This situation is known as a **memory leak**.

Oberon run-time environments usually provide automatic deallocation of the heap; this is known as **garbage collection**. When an anonymous record in no longer referenced by any pointers, it comes under the jurisdiction of the garbage collector. The garbage collector frees these anonymous variables that are no longer in use.

In a garbage-collected environment, a programmer just has to reinitialize a pointer variable—make another call to NEW or set the pointer's value to NIL. If there are no other pointers referencing that location, the garbage collector will eventually free that memory (the memory normally isn't freed instantaneously—collection is triggered by some event or occurs in cycles),

```
NEW(car);   (* first allocation of a CarRec *)
NEW(car);   (* another CarRec is allocated, memory from
              the first allocation can be garbage
              collected *)
car := NIL; (* The second CarRec can be garbage
              collected *)
```

15.4 Pointers and Type Extension

In Oberon, a pointer variable cannot point to arbitrary variables; it must point to a specific array or record type, which is named in its declaration. The pointer type is said to be *bound to* the referenced object's type. So, even though the actual value of a pointer is simply an address, pointers of different types cannot be assigned to one another.

However, recall the notion of record extension and subtypes; extended record types can be assigned to variables of base record types. Similarly, extended pointer types are *compatible* with base pointer types. That is,

```
TYPE
    Point = POINTER TO PointRec;
    PointRec = RECORD
        x, y: REAL
    END;

    Point3D = POINTER TO Point3DRec;
    Point3DRec = RECORD (PointRec)
        z: REAL
    END;

VAR p: Point; p3D: Point3D;
...
    NEW(p3D);
    p3D.x := 3.0; p3D.y := 4.0; p3D.z := 5.0;
    (* initialize the record pointed to by p3D *)

    p := p3D;(* p and p3D point to the same record *)
```

Recall that pointer-to-pointer assignments do not change the values of the records they point to. This is still true when assigning a pointer of extended type to one of the base type. The variable p points to an object with type Point3DRec; that record still has all of the fields x, y, and z. The record itself hasn't changed, but now we can access it through p.

There is a slight complication, though: What does p.z mean? The variable p is supposed to point to a PointRec, and PointRecs don't have a z field. We need some way to state, "This really points to a Point3Drec." That is, how can we move from a static view of p (the type of p itself never changes) to a dynamic view (at different times, p may actually point to different subtypes), and take the actual run-time state of p into account?

The mechanism Oberon provides to do this is called a *type guard*. A **type guard** asserts that a variable's true, current type—its dynamic type—is appropriate for the specified use. The type guard verifies that the variable is being used correctly. The statement,

```
p(Point3D);
```

means, "At this time, the variable p really points to a record of type Point3D." The dynamic type—the type of the object p currently points to—is placed in parentheses after the identifier p. By using the type guard, we can treat p just as though it had been defined as Point3D; then we can dereference the field z,

```
p(Point3D).z := 7.5;
```

Type guards may be performed on either pointers or, if necessary, on variable parameters of record type. The variable must be of the specified type or one of its subtypes.

What happens if the dynamic type is not what the type guard claims it to be? What if p currently points to a PointRec? The type guard is an *assertion* that the current type of p is Point3D. If this assertion is false, the type guard has failed, and the program produces a trap at run time.

Because of this danger of producing a trap, and also to make the use of type guards more versatile, Oberon provides a way to determine the dynamic type of a pointer at run-time. This is called a **type test**. The relational operator 'IS' forms a boolean expression,

```
p IS Point3D
```

This expression evaluates to TRUE if p is currently of type Point3D (or an extension of Point3D). It evaluates to FALSE if p is currently of any other type. If p is equal to NIL, then the result is undefined by the Oberon language (which means the result will depend on your particular compiler—usually this causes a trap).

This gives us the ability to check the type of p before applying a type guard, so we can be sure that the guard is applied to the appropriate type,

```
IF p IS Point3D THEN
    p(Point3D).z := 2.25;
END;
```

Type tests can also be used to control program flow by allowing us to select a processing path based on type,

```
IF p IS Point4D THEN
    (* special 4D processing *)
ELSIF p IS Point3D THEN
```

```
        (* special 3D processing *)
    ELSE
        (* exception conditions *)
    END; (* IF *)
```

Just like type guards, the variable being tested must be a pointer or a variable parameter of record type, and must exactly match the type being tested for or be an extension of that type.

Pascal and Modula-2 have a language feature called variant records. Variant records are a means to provide specialization of types. Oberon does away with variant records because type extension is a safer and more flexible way to accomplish the same goal. The type test is a means of distinguishing between each "variant."

Let us take a closer look at how this "specialization" via subtypes can work,

```
MODULE OfeTypetest;
(* To demonstrate the use of type tests and guards *)

    IMPORT Out;

    TYPE
    (* Declare related types - Luxury and Economy are
        "specializations" of Car *)
      Car* = POINTER TO CarRec;
      CarRec* = RECORD
         year: INTEGER;
         make: ARRAY 12 OF CHAR;
         price: REAL
      END;

      Luxury* = POINTER TO LuxuryRec;
      LuxuryRec = RECORD (CarRec)
         packageCode-: INTEGER
      END;

      Economy* = POINTER TO EconomyRec;
      EconomyRec = RECORD (CarRec)
         rebateAmount-: REAL
      END;

      CarArray = ARRAY 4 OF Car;

    PROCEDURE InitCar*(c: Car; year: INTEGER;
                       make: ARRAY OF CHAR; price: REAL);
    (* Set initial values for type Car *)
    BEGIN
       c.year := year;
```

```
      COPY(make, c.make);
      c.price := price;
  END InitCar;

  PROCEDURE InitLux*(l: Luxury; year: INTEGER;
                     make: ARRAY OF CHAR; price: REAL;
                     packCode: INTEGER);
  (* Set initial values for type Luxury *)
  BEGIN
      InitCar(l, year, make, price);
      l.packageCode := packCode;
  END InitLux;

  PROCEDURE InitEcon*(e: Economy; year: INTEGER;
                      make: ARRAY OF CHAR; price: REAL;
                      rebate: REAL);
  (* Set initial values for type Economy *)
  BEGIN
      InitCar(e, year, make, price);
      e.rebateAmount := rebate
  END InitEcon;

  PROCEDURE Display*(c: Car);
  (* Display Car, Luxury, and Economy field values *)
  BEGIN
      Out.Int(c.year, 0); Out.Ln;
      Out.String(c.make); Out.Ln;
      Out.Real(c.price, 0); Out.Ln;
      IF c IS Luxury THEN
         Out.Int(c(Luxury).packageCode, 0); Out.Ln
      ELSIF c IS Economy THEN
         Out.Real(c(Economy).rebateAmount, 0); Out.Ln
      END; (* IF *)
  END Display;

  PROCEDURE Test*;
  (* To test the declared types and their procedures *)
      VAR arr: CarArray; l: Luxury; e: Economy;
          i: INTEGER;
  BEGIN
      NEW(l);
      InitLux(l, 1996, "Lexus", 40000.00, 3);
      arr[0] := l;
      NEW(l);
      InitLux(l, 1995, "Lincoln", 100000.00, 5);
```

```
        arr[1] := 1;
        NEW(e);
        InitEcon(e, 1994, "Toyota", 20000.00, 600.0);
        arr[2] := e;
        NEW(e);
        InitEcon(e, 1996, "Chevy", 15000.00, 400.0);
        arr[3] := e;
        FOR i := 0 TO 3 DO
            Display(arr[i]); Out.Ln
        END; (* FOR *)
    END Test;


END OfeTypetest.
```

Module OfeTypetest demonstrates a number of important points. We have declared a number of interrelated types: Car and CarRec, Luxury and LuxuryRec, Economy and EconomyRec. This example shows the typical Oberon-2 style—the pointer type is a *reference* to the "object," whereas the associated record type is a *description* of that "object."

Extensions are performed on the description (recall that only record types may be extended) rather than on the "object" itself.

We have also declared CarArray as an array of Car. An array of type CarArray can therefore be used to keep track of a number of Cars. From the notion of subtypes, this means that such an array can also be used to hold objects of type Luxury and Economy. We don't have to define separate arrays—the same array can hold all kinds of Car.

Each car type has its own initialization procedure. However, notice that there is only one display procedure. Display has been made *generic* in that it can display information for any type of car. The type tests and associated type guards enable us to display specific subtype information when it is appropriate.

Could we have done the same thing for the initialization procedures? That is, could we have written one routine to handle all three types? Yes, we could have done so, but the problem is that a generic routine needs to be able to handle all cases; we would have had to declare procedure Init,

```
PROCEDURE Init*(c: Car; year: INTEGER; make: ARRAY OF CHAR;
                price: REAL; packCode: INTEGER;
                rebate: REAL);
```

So, when initializing a variable of type Luxury, the rebate information would be ignored. This could work out relatively well for simple cases, but making Init generic for cases where there are a large number of subtypes could soon become unmanageable and confusing.

As we shall see in chapter 19 on type-bound procedures, Oberon provides another way to define type-specific processing behaviors.

15.5   The WITH Statement

As we saw in procedure OfeTypetest.Display, type tests and type guards may appear together a number of times in a row. So Oberon provides a "short-hand" notation via the WITH statement.

WITH incorporates the type test and type guard together to form a *regional guard*. For example,

```
IF c IS Luxury THEN
    Out.Int(c(Luxury).packageCode, 0); Out.Ln
ELSIF c IS Economy THEN
    Out.Real(c(Economy).rebateAmount, 0); Out.Ln
END; (* IF *)
```

This could be rewritten by using the WITH statement to become,

```
WITH
    c: Luxury DO
        Out.Int(c.packageCode, 0); Out.Ln
|   c: Economy DO
        Out.Real(c.rebateAmount, 0); Out.Ln
END; (* WITH *)
```

The first regional guard that is satisfied executes its associated block of statements. In this respect, the WITH statement is similar to the CASE statement. However, the WITH statement does more than just select alternatives; it applies a type guard to each use of the guarded variable within the block. Notice that we needed to write only c.packageCode within the WITH block; rather than c(Luxury).packageCode.

The general form of the WITH statement is,

```
WITH
    v: T1 DO
        <1st statement sequence; any use of v is type
guarded as T1>
|   v: T2 DO
        <2nd statement sequence; any use of v is type
guarded as T2>
|   v: T3 DO
        <3rd statement sequence; any use of v is type
guarded as T3>
    . . .
ELSE
    <exception sequence>
END
```

In the regional guard v: Tn, the same rules apply as would for the type test v IS Tn and the type guard v(Tn). That is, v must be a pointer or a variable parameter of record type; and v must be of the exact type being tested for or an extension of that type.

As should be expected, the ELSE clause executes if no regional guard is matched. Also note that if no ELSE clause is provided and there is no match, a run-time error occurs. As usual, it is recommended to always have an ELSE alternative.

15.6   Exercises

1. Describe the meanings of the words pointer, location, and address, and then explain their relationships.

2. Why do you think Oberon doesn't let you directly examine or modify a pointer's value? That is, why can't I set my pointer to look at any arbitrary piece of computer memory?

3. What are the advantages of dynamic memory allocation? (That is, what are the advantages of using pointers and NEW?)

4. Explain the meaning of the term "indirection" and how it applies to pointers.

5. Explain the compatibility of NIL with pointer types; also describe the uses of NIL.

6. Explain the difference between assigning to a pointer and through a pointer. Be sure to include an explanation of the dereference operator '^'.

7. Using the Car types declared in this chapter, write a boolean function IsEquals that returns TRUE if the cars being compared contain the *same information* (values). Make sure you handle all types of cars in the comparison.

8. Describe the three kinds of memory management schemes that are normally used by Oberon implementations. Explain why these three types exist and the advantages of each.

9. Describe the uses of type tests and type guards.

10. Explain the sensibility of the Oberon "style" of declaring objects and object descriptions (i.e., pointers and their associated record types). Do you think there could have been a more straightforward way to do it? Explain your answer.

11. Write a procedure that will sort an array of Cars. Luxury cars should come first and Economy cars last. They should be sorted first in alphabetical order by make, then by year and price.

12. Create a Date type (both pointer and an associated record type). Write procedures to initialize the date, to set the date, to display the date (in a variety of formats), and one to change the date by a given number of days (this can be either positive—to give a later date—or negative—to give a previous date).

13. Create a DateAndTime type which extends the Date type from the previous exercise. Add additional procedures to set the time and to change the time by minutes. Don't forget to change the existing procedures to handle the extended type.

Chapter 16
Uses of Pointers

16.1 Why Use Pointers?

Because pointer types are such an important part of the Oberon language, and the fact that many people initially find pointers to be confusing, a separate chapter is provided on some of the more common and appropriate uses for pointers. Later in chapter 19 on type-bound procedures, we will see another important use of pointers.

There are several reasons why dynamic allocation of records via pointers is advantageous. By using pointers, dynamic structures can be built. These dynamic structures are similar to arrays, but more flexible. Arrays and records are static; they maintain the same size and structure during their whole existence. By using dynamic structures, we are able to separate the logical order from the physical limitations. These structures can grow and shrink during the execution of a program.

We can also use pointers as procedure arguments, and as the result type of functions. Also, pointers can be used to create open array types.

In the next sections, we will take a closer look at these applications of pointers.

16.2 Dynamic Structures and Lists

One reason that pointers are such a powerful feature is that they may point to records that also contain pointers. Because of this, we can create "links" from one record to the next.

Recall that we have said that dynamic structures may change size as a program runs. They are similar to arrays—but arrays are fixed in size; once an array is created, it will have the same number of elements for its entire lifetime.

Dynamic structures, on the other hand, are able to grow and shrink during run-time via use of links (pointers) and repeated calls to NEW(). These kinds of structures generally consist of two parts: nodes and links. A node contains data. A link ties one node to the next node (via a pointer).

Let us take a look at an example:

```
TYPE
    Node = POINTER TO NodeDesc;
    NodeDesc = RECORD
               data: DataType;
               link: Node
    END;

VAR
    list: Node;
```

Type Node is declared as a pointer to a record—exactly like other pointer declarations we have already seen. Remember that we can think of the pointer as referring to the "object" and the record as the "description" of that object. Note that this example uses a common Oberon naming convention: the "object name" (Node) with "Desc" appended to it (NodeDesc).

The field data can be of any type, including other record or pointer types. In fact, we could have any number of data fields in our record, depending on what information you want to store within the node.

The field link has type Node; and a Node object points to a NodeDesc, which means link can be used to point to the next node. The link can be used to tie this record to another record. In effect, this forms a chain (or linked list) of records.

In order to make use of our node type, a variable list is defined, which is used as the starting place for a list of nodes.

How do we use list?

First of all, we should initialize our list—it should start out "empty." It has no nodes to which it points, which means it has no elements yet. As we said before, some Oberon implementations automatically initialize pointers to NIL, but we will make sure of this by doing the initialization ourselves.

```
list := NIL;
```

NIL is normally used to mark the end of linked structures. We can test list to see if it is empty by comparing it to NIL:

```
IF list = NIL THEN ...
(* if this is true, then the list is empty *)
```

In fact, since this is potentially an operation we perform often, we can create a function that tests a list for "emptiness":

```
PROCEDURE IsEmpty(list: Node): BOOLEAN;
BEGIN
    IF list = NIL THEN
        RETURN TRUE
    ELSE
        RETURN FALSE
    END;
```

```
END IsEmpty;
```

Now the test becomes,

```
IF IsEmpty(list) THEN ...
```

which doesn't seem to save us much effort. However, because we have defined it as a function, we can effectively hide the implementation. That is, if the implementation of our list changes, we don't have to change the interface; we can still use the function IsEmpty().

Recall the notions of abstraction and encapsulation; our goal is to create an abstract data type—the data type along with operations to perform on that data. What other operations might we want for our list?

We would probably want a way to add elements to the list, such as

```
PROCEDURE Add*(VAR list: Node; item: Node);
BEGIN
    item.next := list;
    list := item
END Add;
```

This operation would add an item to the beginning of the list. That is, the next field for item is set to point to the old list (which works even if the list is empty—item.next would then be set to NIL). Then we set the list to point at the new first node (item).

Procedure Add assumes that you have allocated item somewhere (a NEW() operation is performed sometime before the call to Add is made). At the beginning of Add, item looks like,

That is, item points to a Node, which contains data, and a next field (which points to NIL).

If we started with an empty list,

Procedure Add does two things: it makes item.next point to the start of the list (this effectively doesn't change anything the first time through because the list was NIL already); then it makes list point to item (item becomes the first element on the list). So now our picture is

What if, instead, list wasn't empty to start with (it has at least one Node already),

* This list could continue on indefinitely with more Nodes.

In this case, procedure Add will make `item.next` point to the same node as `list`, and then make `list` point to `item`s node,

Both pointers, `item` and `list`, then point to the same node.

Because our list is dynamic, we can Add as many new items as we want. But then we should have a way to remove items:

```
PROCEDURE Remove(VAR list, item: Node);
BEGIN
    IF list = NIL THEN
        item := NIL
    ELSE
        item := list;
        list := list.next;
        item.next := NIL
    END;
END Remove;
```

If the list is empty, `item` comes back set to NIL. Otherwise, `item` is the first Node on the list. And then the list points to the next Node on the list.

This section is not intended to be a comprehensive guide to lists and dynamic data structures. The intention is only to introduce the idea of using pointers to create dynamic structures (such linked structures are sometimes called **recursive structures**—recursive meaning something that refers to itself). There are many other sources, which cover this topic in greater detail. However, there are several points to make before moving on.

First, after a node (or other record) is allocated with NEW(), the only way to reference it is with pointers (through its links). Be careful not to "lose" the list or items on the list. For example, if assignments are done incorrectly, there many not be any pointers left to a particular node. Once such a record is lost, there is no way to get it back; and the record is free to be garbage collected.

When a dynamically allocated record is no longer referenced by any pointers, it is (eventually) deallocated automatically. As we said before, the programmer doesn't need to worry about freeing memory—when a record is no longer needed, the system gets rid of it. So for our list, if we wanted to clear the list, we don't need to remove every node. Simply stating,

```
list := NIL;
```

clears the list and all "lost" nodes are automatically deallocated by the garbage collector.

Second, most Oberon environments provide a way to "turn off" garbage collection and allow the programmer to manually free memory. In those situations, a special operation is provided—usually in the SYSTEM module (for example, SYSTEM.Dispose()). However, for most programming situations, it is better to let the garbage collector deal with deallocation.

Finally, it is permissible and often desirable to have more than one pointer referencing a single record. In fact, it is often necessary to use temporary pointers when performing operations on lists.

16.3   Pointers as Parameters and Return Values of Functions

We have already seen some examples of pointers being passed as parameters to procedures. This is useful when your data types have been defined in terms of pointers.

Because the pointer's value is really a location, an address is really being passed; that is, a reference to a structure rather than the structure itself. Operations can be more efficient this way, especially if you are passing large structures such as arrays as value parameters. Passing a pointer to an array is usually more efficient than passing the array itself.

Remember that arguments passed as value parameters are copied, which is why we usually pass arrays as variable parameters. Passing a pointer to an array is an alternative to using value parameters.

You need to be aware when passing pointers that the location's value can *always* be changed, even if a pointer is declared as a value parameter. Changes to the values accessed through the pointer are permanent.

However, changing the value of the pointer itself—changing the location it points to—isn't permanent when using value parameters. A copy of the pointer is made when it is passed as a value parameter.

Pointers may be also used as return values for functions. Recall that Oberon doesn't permit structured types (arrays and records) to be used as return values of functions. Using pointers to structures as return values is a way to get around this restriction.

16.4   Pointers and Open Arrays

Recall how we used open arrays as parameters, which eliminated the need to specify the length of the array. This helped make a procedure more generic; we could then pass arrays of various sizes to the procedure.

It is also possible to declare open arrays as pointer types. As with other pointer types, procedure NEW is used to create an instance of the open array. Also, recall how dereferencing of a record field is implied when it is accessed through a pointer variable,

> `list.next` is the same as `list^.next`

Similarly, array elements accessed through a pointer to an array don't require the use of the '^' operator,

> `arrPtr[i]` is the same as `arrPtr^[i]`

The following is an example of how we might use a pointer type with an open array,

```
TYPE
    ArrayPtr = POINTER TO ARRAY OF LONGINT;

PROCEDURE Do*;
    VAR i: LONGINT; arr: ArrayPtr;
BEGIN
    NEW(arr, 20); (* Length of the array is 20 *)

    FOR i := 0 TO LEN(arr^) -1 DO
    (* Note the "^" is required for dereferencing the
        entire array *)
        arr[i]   :=   i;   (*   But   not   when   accessing
                                individual elements *)
    END; (* FOR *)
. . .
END Do;
```

The statement NEW(arr, 20) creates an anonymous integer array of length 20, which is referenced through `arr`.

Multidimensional arrays can be created the same way:

```
TYPE
    Matrix = POINTER TO ARRAY OF ARRAY OF REAL;

VAR m: Matrix;
. . .

NEW(m, 4, 5);       (* Creates a 4 x 5 matrix *)
```

Open arrays allow the programmer to specify array size bounds at run-time. This can give an advantage similar to dynamic structures—making arrays more flexible.

16.5 Exercises

1. Compare and contrast the use of arrays versus dynamic structures such as lists.

2. If Oberon did not provide garbage collection, how would you clear a list (such as the list defined in this chapter) so as not to cause a memory leak? Assuming you had a procedure Dispose(p), where p is the object to be deallocated, write a procedure to clear a list.

3. Explain the term *recursive structure* and why it applies to lists.

4. Rewrite the Remove procedure in this chapter so that it is instead a function that returns a Node.

5. Create an open array type that acts just like the list described in this chapter. Write procedures to initialize the array, clear it, add elements, and remove elements. What problems do you face to make an open array mimic a truly dynamic structure?

6. Create a list structure whose nodes contain Car data (see chapter 15 for Car type declarations). Write a boolean function that will search the list for a particular make and year of car, and return TRUE if the car is found on the list.

7. A stack is a structure whose elements can be accessed only in a last-in-first-out (LIFO) manner. This means that only the most recently inserted element can be removed. Create a Stack type that holds characters as its data. Write the following procedures, which operate on a Stack:

    a. Push—adds an element to the stack.
    b. Pop—removes an element from the stack.
    c. Clear—empties the stack.
    d. IsEmpty—boolean function returns TRUE if the stack is empty.

    Then, using the Stack type you have just created, write a procedure that will reverse a string passed to it.

Chapter 17
Sets

17.1 Using Sets

This may seem an odd place to discuss one of Oberon's basic types; after all, we talked about all the other basic types toward the beginning of the book. Sets serve some unique purposes in Oberon, and so this topic deserves enough attention to warrant a separate chapter.

Sets are similar to sets from mathematics, only in Oberon, they are in some ways more limited (then again, in some ways they might be considered more powerful).

Sets are useful because they can hold more than one value at a time, and each value is unique within a set—that is, values cannot be repeated.

A SET in Oberon may be used to represent the sets of integers between 0 and MAX(SET). A SET may contain any or all of those values (or none of those values) at the same time. MAX(SET) is dependent on the implementation. MAX(SET) is normally based on the *word size* of a computer system, measured in bits, which would mean,

```
MAX(SET) = <word size> - 1
```

So on a 32-bit system, MAX(SET) has a value of 31.

Let us look at an example:

```
MODULE OfeSet;

(* Demonstrate the use of sets *)

   IMPORT Out;

   PROCEDURE Do*;
      VAR s: SET; i, each: INTEGER;
      (* Define a set variable *)
   BEGIN
      s := {1, 4, 9, 16, 25};
      (* Initialize the set to contain the values 1, 4, 9,
         16 and 25 *)
```

```
FOR i := 0 TO MAX(SET) DO
    IF i IN s THEN
    (* if i is a member of the set *)
        Out.Int(i, 0); Out.Ln   (* write it out *)
    END; (* IF *)
END; (* FOR *)
Out.Ln
END Do;
```

```
END OfeSet.
```

As with any other type, we can define variables of type SET. In this case, we have defined a variable s. The first statement within the procedure,

```
s := {1, 4, 9, 16, 25};
```

is an assignment statement used to initialize set s. Notice that assignment of set values requires the use of curly brackets '{ }' which enclose a comma-separated list of integer values. The bracketed expression is known as a **set constructor**, which defines the value of a set by listing its elements between curly brackets. We can then say that the values 1, 4, 9, 16, and 25 are elements of the set s.

We could have also used the range operator '..' in the set constructor,

```
s := {1, 10 .. 15, 20};
```

which would assign the values 1, 10, 11, 12, 13, 14, 15, and 20 to set s.

The FOR loop that follows is used to demonstrate another set operator; IN is used to test whether a particular value is an element of the set. If i IN s is TRUE, then the value i is written to the log.

After running OfeSet.Do, you should see the following output:

```
1
4
9
16
25
```

17.2   Sets and Boolean Relations

We have already seen one type of boolean relation used on a set. The relation IN tells us whether a particular value is an element of a set. The general form is

```
<value> IN <set expression>
```

An IN expression evaluates to TRUE if the value is one of the elements of the set represented by the <set expression>. The <set expression> can be any expression of set type: a set constructor, a set variable, a set constant, and so forth.

The only other relational operators that can be used on sets are '=' and '#'. Two sets are equal if they include the same elements (i.e., each contains the same values as their elements). Note also that two empty sets are considered as being equal to one another. The following are a few examples, for sets s and t:

```
s := {1, 2, 3, 4, 5}
t := {1, 2, 3, 4}
IF t = s THEN ...          (* FALSE *)
```

This evaluates to FALSE because s and t don't contain all the same elements.

```
IF t # s THEN ...          (* TRUE *)
```

This evaluates to TRUE because s and t contain different elements.

```
t := {1, 2, 3, 4, 5}
IF t = s THEN ...          (* TRUE *)
```

Sets s and t have the same elements, so t = s evaluates to TRUE now.

```
s := { }; t := { };
IF t = s THEN ...          (* TRUE *)
```

Both s and t are empty sets, so this evaluates to TRUE.

17.3   Other Set Operators

There are a number of operators that can be used on sets. The symbols are familiar, but have somewhat different meanings when applied to sets: +, *, −, and /.

The '+' operator produces the *union* of two sets. A **union** is an expression that evaluates to a set that contains all the members of both sets. (*Note*: the same value never appears more than once within a set, so that if a particular value appears in both sets, it still appears only once in the resulting set.) Assume s, t, and u are defined as set variables:

```
s := {1, 2, 3, 4, 5};
t := {2, 4, 6, 8};
u := s + t;
(* u now contains all the elements that were in both s
      and t. That is, 1, 2, 3, 4, 5, 6, and 8 *)
```

The '*' operator produces the *intersection* of two sets. An **intersection** is an expression that evaluates to a set that contains all values that belong to both sets; that is, values *common* to both sets.

```
s := {1, 2, 3, 4, 5};
```

```
t := {2, 4, 6, 8};
u := s * t;
(* u now contains all the elements that were common to
   s and t. That is, 2 and 4 *)
```

The '−' operator produces *set difference*. **Set difference** is an expression that evaluates to a set that contains all the members of the first set that are not also members of the second set. That is, *remove* the values of the second set if they are present in the first set,

```
s := {1, 2, 3, 4, 5};
t := {2, 4, 6, 8};
u := s - t; (* u now contains 1, 3, and 5. *)
```

The '/' operator produces the *symmetric difference* of two sets. **Symmetric difference** is an expression that evaluates to a set that contains elements belonging to one set or the other, but not both. If a particular value appears in both sets, then it is excluded from the result:

```
s := {1, 2, 3, 4, 5};
t := {2, 4, 6, 8};
u := s / t;
(* u now contains 1, 3, 5, 6, and 8. The values 2 and
   4 appear in both s and t and so are not assigned to
   u *)
```

Recall Oberon's precedence rules (as with arithmetic operators); '*' and '/' have precedence over '+' and '−'. Thus,

```
s + t * u    =>    s + (t * u)
s - t / u    =>    s - (t / u)
```

Notice that when a minus sign appears in front of a set, the result is the set of all integers between 0 and MAX(SET) that are not elements of s; this is called the **set complement**. That is, assuming MAX(SET) is 31,

```
-s  means the same as  {0 .. 31} - s
```

Because '−' has lower precedence than '*' and '/', even when it is used to mean set complement, parentheses are generally required within set expressions for set complement:

```
s *  -t
(* ERROR! The compiler expects '*' to be followed by a
   set, not another operator *)


s * (-t)
(* OK. Parentheses force '-t' to be evaluated first *)
```

Some related terminology you might encounter is listed below:

- A **subset** of a set may contain elements only of the given set. (Note that a set is also a subset of itself.)
- A **proper subset** of a set must contain fewer elements than the whole set.
- **Disjoint** sets cannot contain any elements in common.

Examples of the two most common uses for sets in Oberon are provided in the next few sections.

17.4   Sets as Flags

There are many times when we need to keep track of some condition or *state* within a program. Boolean variables are often used for this purpose. Such variables used to represent program conditions are often called **state variables**. State variables can be used to identify exception conditions or otherwise control the flow of a program.

Many times, a single boolean variable isn't enough to represent all the states that we wish to track. When a number of states must be simultaneously monitored, each state is often referred to as a **flag**. We could perhaps use an array of boolean variables—one variable to stand for each flag—but sets are already defined to hold multiple values all at once. So, let us see how a set can be used to hold flags.

The following is a partial listing of a module that implements some sort of game.

```
MODULE OfeGame;

(* An incomplete module that demonstrates sets as flags *)

   IMPORT ...

   CONST
      beginner* = 0; intermediate* = 1; expert* = 2;
      sound* = 3; mouse* = 4; joystick* = 5;

   VAR
      options-: SET;

   PROCEDURE Start*;
   (* To start the game *)
      VAR i: INTEGER;
   BEGIN
      options := {beginner, sound, mouse};
      (* options is initialized *)

      ...
```

```
      IF sound IN options THEN
      (* if the sound option is "turned on" *)
         InitSoundCard
      END;  (* IF *)

      IF mouse IN options THEN
      (* if the mouse option is "turned on" *)
         DetectMouseDriver
      END;  (* IF *)

      BeginGame

   END Start;

   PROCEDURE ToggleOption*(opt: INTEGER);
   (* To set or reset the option 'opt' in 'options' *)
   BEGIN
      options := options / {opt};
   END ToggleOption;

   ... (* other procedures *)

END OfeGame.
```

In OfeGame, we set up constants to reflect the various options or flags available. Then we define a set variable `options`, which keeps track of the current options selected. By using IN we can test whether that option is "on," and by using other set operations, we can turn these options (or flags) "on" or "off" as needed.

In OfeGame.Start, the "flags" list is initialized; set to the game "default options." The default settings are for a beginner player with sound turned on and mouse input enabled,

```
      options := {beginner, sound, mouse};
```

Then, later on, we can test for these options if we need to perform special processing, say initializing the sound card if sound is turned on, or checking for the presence of a mouse driver.

```
      IF sound IN options THEN
         InitSoundCard
      END;  (* IF *)
```

Also notice the procedure called ToggleOption. Can you tell what it does? "Toggling" means switching between two choices. In this case, each option can be either "on" or "off." ToggleOption will turn an option "on" if it was "off," or it will turn the option "off" if it was "on." For example, say we started with options as noted above, that is, sound is "on," then

```
ToggleOption(sound);
```

would then turn sound "off." That is, the value of options would be {beginner, mouse}.

If we were to call ToggleOption(sound) again, then sound would be turned back "on" (i.e., options = {beginner, sound, mouse}).

All sorts of states can be tracked in this manner. You could keep track of program exception conditions, attributes of a collection of data, windowing "styles" for how a window is displayed on the computer screen (e.g., is there a border, are scrollbars permitted) and so forth.

17.5   Sets for Bit Manipulation

Even though Oberon is a high-level computer language, there are times when low-level operations need to be performed. For instance, sometimes you may need to change values one bit at a time.

Recall that a computer's basic unit of understanding is a binary digit, or bit. Bits have a value of either 0 or 1.

Every piece of information a digital computer represents is actually composed of bits. Bits are usually grouped together to form *bytes* and *words*. **Bytes** can be used to represent characters, whereas **words** are often used to represent integers (this may seem backwards, but these are "old" computer terms).

An in-depth discussion on low-level programming is beyond the scope of this book; however, a short overview of how to manipulate computer information on the bit level is included here. This is called **bit manipulation** or sometimes *bitwise operations*.

First, let us discuss why sets can be used for bit manipulation. It has to do with the fact that, in Oberon, a set is implemented as a computer *word*. Operations on words are generally very efficient. When a computer is called a "32-bit" computer, it can deal with information in "32-bit"-sized chunks. So in that case, a word is 32 bits long.

On a 32-bit computer, a set would be implemented as a chunk of 32 bits; that is, as a computer word. The set would then be able to contain up to 32 different values—one bit per value—which would give a range for the set from 0 to 31.

A value is included as an element of the set if that particular bit is turned "on"; that is, the bit has a value of 1. A value isn't an element of the set if that bit is turned "off"; that is, has a value of 0. So since a set variable s is represented by a word, if we assign s := { }, all bits are assigned the value of 0:

31	30	29	28	27	26	25	24	23	22	21	20	19	18	17	16
0	0	0	0	0	0	0	0	0	0	0	0	0	0	0	0

15	14	13	12	11	10	9	8	7	6	5	4	3	2	1	0
0	0	0	0	0	0	0	0	0	0	0	0	0	0	0	0

Now, suppose we assign s := {0, 5, 12}. What happens?

15	14	13	12	11	10	9	8	7	6	5	4	3	2	1	0
0	0	0	1	0	0	0	0	0	0	1	0	0	0	0	1

The bits at positions 0, 5, and 12 all now have the value 1.

So, by using our various set operations, we can turn bits on and off, as well as test the state of each bit (check if it is on or off).

To turn every bit off, we just assign the empty set,

```
s := { };
```

To turn every bit on, we assign all the values from 0 through 31,

```
s := {0 .. 31};
```

To test whether a particular bit is on, use the IN operator. For example, to check whether the bit in the sixth position is on,

```
IF 5 IN s THEN ...
```

To change individual bits, use the '+' and '–' operators (or alternately, the standard procedures INCL() and EXCL()),

```
s := s + {0, 4};
(* turns on the 0th and fourth bits *)

INCL(s, 3); (* turns on the third bit *)

s := s - {16, 20};
(* turns off the sixteenth and twentieth bits *)

EXCL(s, 31); (* turns off the thirty-first bit *)
```

To reverse all current bit states,

```
s := {0 .. 31} - s; (* from the set of all bits, turn
                       off the ones that were in s *)

s := -s;            (* same as {0 .. 31} - s *)
```

When might you want to do bit manipulation? When programming at the operating system level (sometimes called "systems programming") may require it. Programming *device drivers* or other types of problems that deal closely with computer hardware may require it as well. Also, reading data or calling procedures written in other computer languages sometimes requires "bit-level" control.

17.6 Exercises

1. Explain why SET is a basic type in Oberon. Can you think of alternative ways of providing the same functionality? Describe an alternate scheme that could take the place of the SET type. Make sure to include potential problems with your proposed scheme.

2. Decide whether the following are valid relations and then determine if they evaluate to TRUE or FALSE. Assume s and t are SETs and,

```
s := {1, 3, 5, 7, 11, 13, 17, 19, 23, 29, 31};
t := {1, 4, 9, 16, 25};
```

   a. s = t
   b. s # t
   c. s # { }
   d. {9} IN t
   e. 9 IN t
   f. ~(17 IN s)
   g. t # {1, 4, 16, 25}
   h. { } IN s

3. Evaluate the following expressions (make sure you take precedence into account). Assume s, t, u, and v are SETs and,

```
s := {1, 3, 5, 7, 11, 13, 17, 19, 23, 29, 31};
t := {1, 4, 9, 16, 25};
u := { };
v := {0 .. 31};
```

   a. s + t * v
   b. u * t + t * s
   c. s / t + u - v
   d. v - u + t / s
   e. s + t - s / u * v
   f. -s * (s + t) / (v - u) * u
   g. s * (-t) / s * t / (-s)
   h. v - s + t / u

4. Create a Font type that describes attributes on characters that are to be displayed within a word processor. Attributes should include size and style (e.g. bold, italics, and underline) information. How should you represent each of these attributes?

5. Write a module that can manipulate sets of characters. That is, it can perform all the set operations (union, intersection, tests for inclusion) on a set composed of the entire ASCII character set. Create a CharSet type and write procedures to perform all of the set operations on it. (*Hint*: Use an ARRAY n OF SET.)

6. Suppose you wanted to perform bit-level manipulation on INTEGERs. What problems would you encounter with the way Oberon treats INTEGERs? Can you use Oberon's SET type to help? Explain your answer in detail.

Part III

Type-bound Procedures

Chapter 18
Objects

18.1 Modular Program Design

Thus far in this book, we have demonstrated the use of modular design when writing programs. Discussions on abstraction and encapsulation were intended to show how to effectively use Oberon's module construct to this end.

Modules are used to provide structure to a program. A program can be divided into independent units, each containing information and operations specific to a particular task. Global variables can be used to hold values needed for the entire time the module is active. Types, variables, and procedures can be exported to be used in other modules.

Modular design provides **information hiding**—another term for encapsulation. Interface definitions specify what is accessible to client modules, whereas implementation details are hidden. In this way, software systems can be developed by multiple programmers, each creating modules independently.

Modular design encourages the creation of abstract data types. The structure of the data isn't visible outside of the module; it can be created and changed only by a set of exported procedures. Only its essential properties are known—not its implementation.

The operations on an abstract data type can be carefully designed and programmed once, and then used over and over again. The data are protected—they cannot be tampered with in ways not intended by the module designer.

Implementation details are hidden, and little or no documentation about the implementation needs to be provided to users of the module. Only the interface needs documentation, and this is facilitated by choosing meaningful variable and parameter names.

The implementation is free to change without affecting any importing modules. In fact, it is possible to substitute different implementations; and none of the client modules will have to be modified (or in many environments, even recompiled), as long as the interface remains the same.

Providing proper structure, through modularization and abstraction, is key to making programs understandable and reliable. A program must be decomposed into pieces that can be considered one at a time. These smaller pieces can be understood separately without having to consider the whole problem at once.

Connection between the pieces (modules) should be simple and straightforward. Related modules should interact through those interfaces only.

A particular module may be simply a collection of exported procedures with no internal data at all. A mathematical library—containing functions to calculate square root, sine, cosine, and so forth—would be an example of this.

A module could also provide data on which it operates. Little or nothing is known about how the data are represented. Procedures must be called in order to operate on it; this is called an **abstract data structure**. Module Out is an example of an abstract data structure.

Finally, the module might not have data of its own, but instead provide a data type from which multiple instances can be created. Again, procedures are provided to operate on this data type. We call this an abstract data type; the List type and other dynamic structures are examples of this.

We could easily create useful and reliable software using the features of modular design. Modula-2 has been used for many years to do just that. But there is something that Oberon provides in addition to all of that—the concept of extensibility. Extensibility allows us to take a single general solution, and apply it in other more specific situations. As we have seen, the notion of subtypes permits us to extend types in this manner. In the next section, we examine this further.

18.2   Introduction to Programming with Objects

Oberon not only supports modular design, but also extensible design. Extensible, in this case, is synonymous with what most people call *object-oriented*. However, the term object-oriented has been overused to the point of serious confusion to many people—even experienced programmers.

The purveyors of object-oriented programming introduced new terminology unfamiliar to most programmers, although many of the concepts were, in fact, the same as or very similar to "traditional" methodologies.

Oberon's designers wished to keep familiar terminology for these "new" programming concepts. When compared to Modula-2, the only truly new facilities were type-extension and type-bound procedures.

Depending on whom you talk to, there are any number of definitions as to exactly what is required for object-oriented programming. For the most part, it seems to break down into three main characteristics:

- data abstraction
- inheritance
- dynamic binding

As we have already seen, data abstraction is provided by the module construct in Oberon.

Type extension, which we also have discussed, provides inheritance. Inheritance is another term describing subtype relationships.

Finally, what is dynamic binding? With type extension, base types are used to create extended types—this forms the subtype relationship. But procedures must be written to explicitly handle each type. Either a separate procedure must be written for each type, or type tests must be performed within a procedure to ensure proper handling of each type. In either case, the programmer is responsible for keeping track of which "version" is used.

As we shall see in the next chapter, type-bound procedures allow us to redefine the actions associated with a base type, so that they may operate properly on an extended type. Type-bound procedures free the programmer from having to explicitly handle each type; the appropriate procedure is called based on the dynamic type of the caller.

This is what is meant by dynamic binding—an appropriate procedure is bound (called) at run-time by examining the dynamic type of the caller. That is, the specific action to be performed is determined at run-time, as opposed to static binding, which takes place at compile-time.

Because we are now aware of these characteristics, the term "object" will have a more precise meaning. An **object** is an instance of an abstract data type with dynamic binding of its procedures.

In extensible design, the emphasis changes from writing isolated procedures to structuring modules around types of objects where whole data structures and their associated operations can be reused *together*.

We concern ourselves with data and its operations. Recall that for abstract data types, we spoke of primitive operations—those operations that required knowledge of the data type's implementation. Now we can consider what typical primitive operations might be declared for objects.

- Construction—allocating and initializing an object.
- Inspection—examining the data values the object contains.
- Modification—setting the data values the object contains.
- Iteration—processing collections (arrays, lists, etc.) of objects.
- Status—examining the state of the object (is it in a valid state?).

The preceding discussion of objects is by no means all inclusive; even though we will see some of these notions in action in the next chapter. But since Oberon's object-oriented terminology differs somewhat from the "standard" terminology, let us briefly look at how these terms correspond to one another.

By now, you should be familiar with Oberon's concept of type. This generally corresponds to the term **class** in standard object terminology; that is, class as in "classification." The intention of this word is to imply subtype hierarchy relationships.

However, class is a broader term than type—they aren't *quite* the same thing. That is, the class construct provides:

- a mechanism for encapsulation
- an object's structure
- an object's behavior

Oberon models these concepts separately; encapsulation is provided by modules, structure comes from the type mechanism, and behavior is described, as we shall see, by *dynamically bound* procedures.

The term **object** is synonymous with variable, and a **method** is the same as a type-bound procedure. Standard object terminology refers to a *message being passed to an object*—which is equivalent to a procedure call. (This is not *exactly* true; message passing differs from a procedure call in some respects. But for most common uses, they are equivalent.)

Polymorphism is another term closely associated with dynamic binding. A polymorphic object can assume many different "shapes" at run-time. Operations behave differently depending on the object's current "form."

In order to apply an operation to such an object, the programmer doesn't explicitly distinguish between the various shapes; instead a message is sent telling the object what to do. The object responds to the message by invoking the method (calling a procedure), which implements the operation for that object's actual type.

In preceding chapters, we spoke at length about type extension and sub-type relationships. These notions fall under the heading **inheritance**. Inheritance speaks of *superclasses* (similar to base types) and *subclasses* (extended types).

Hopefully, should you read one of the popular books on object methodologies, these differences in terminology won't hinder your understanding.

18.3   Exercises

1. Describe modular design and explain how Oberon supports it.

2. Explain the meaning of information hiding and why it is an appropriate term.

3. Some people claim that programs should be "self-documenting." Explain what you think that means and how modular design could help with it.

4. Explain data abstraction, inheritance, and dynamic binding. Be sure to give details as to why each is important to extensible (object-oriented) design. That is, what are their benefits?

5. Describe the meaning of the word *object* as it relates to extensible design.

6. Object-oriented programming has been touted as being a more "natural" way to build software. From what you know at this point, do you agree? Support your answer.

Chapter 19
Type-bound Procedures

19.1   Types and Procedures

We have seen how types and procedures work together—types describe information and procedures describe the actions performed on that information. Up to this point, the main way to tie procedures to the information was as arguments to the procedure. But if we wish to define operations for a particular type, is there a better way to tie them together? The following is an example of how that might be done:

```
MODULE OfeTypebound;

(* To demonstrate the use of type-bound procedures *)

   IMPORT In, Out;

   TYPE
      Car* = POINTER TO CarDesc;
      CarDesc* = RECORD
         year: INTEGER;
         make: ARRAY 12 OF CHAR;
         price: REAL
      END;

      Luxury* = POINTER TO LuxuryDesc;
      LuxuryDesc = RECORD (CarDesc)
         packageCode-: INTEGER
      END;

      Economy* = POINTER TO EconomyDesc;
      EconomyDesc = RECORD (CarDesc)
         rebateAmount-: REAL
      END;

      CarArray = ARRAY 10 OF Car;
```

```
PROCEDURE (c: Car) Read*;
(* Use procedures from In to read in data fields for a
   Car *)
BEGIN
   In.Int(c.year);
   In.String(c.make);
   In.Real(c.price);
END Read;

PROCEDURE (l: Luxury) Read*;
(* To read in a Luxury car *)
BEGIN
   l.Read^;     (* Can you guess what this line does? *)
   In.Int(l.packageCode);
END Read;

PROCEDURE (e: Economy) Read*;
(* To read in an Economy car *)
BEGIN
   e.Read^;
   In.Real(e.rebateAmount)
END Read;

PROCEDURE (c: Car) Display*;
(* Use procedures from Out to display fields from a Car *)
BEGIN
   Out.Int(c.year, 0); Out.Ln;
   Out.String(c.make); Out.Ln;
   Out.Real(c.price, 0); Out.Ln;
END Display;

PROCEDURE (l: Luxury) Display*;
(* To display a Luxury car *)
BEGIN
   l.Display^; (* Again, can you guess what this does? *)
   Out.Int(l.packageCode, 0); Out.Ln
END Display;

PROCEDURE (e: Economy) Display*;
(* To display an Economy car *)
BEGIN
   e.Display^;
   Out.Real(e.rebateAmount, 0); Out.Ln
END Display;
```

```
PROCEDURE Do*;
(* Will read in a "database" of cars, and then display
   their information *)
VAR  arr: CarArray;  l: Luxury;  e: Economy;  c: Car;
     recordsRead, i: INTEGER; type: ARRAY 2 OF CHAR;
BEGIN
   In.Open;
   recordsRead := 0;

   In.String(type);       (* The database keeps track of
                             the type of the car *)

   WHILE In.Done & (recordsRead < LEN(arr) ) DO
   (* type is used to create the appropriate car *)

      IF type = "l" THEN
         NEW(l);
         c := l (* After it is created, all cars are
                    handled the same *)
      ELSIF type = "e" THEN
         NEW(e);
         c := e;
      ELSE
         Out.String("ERROR:  Unknown  car  type  found.
                     Ending program.");
         Out.Ln;
         RETURN
      END; (* IF*)

      c.Read;  (* Which procedure is called? *)
      arr[recordsRead] := c; (* All cars are kept in the
                                same array *)
      INC(recordsRead);
      In.String(type);      (* get the type of the next
                             record *)
   END; (* WHILE *)
 (* Display information for all cars in the "database" *)
   FOR i := 0 TO recordsRead-1 DO
      arr[i].Display; Out.Ln
   END; (* FOR *)

END Do;

END OfeTypebound.
```

The module OfeTypebound reimplements the Car type and its subtypes. You can test it on the following data:

```
"l" 1994 "Lincoln" 55000.00 3
"l" 1995 "Cadillac" 65000.00 4
"l" 1996 "Lexus" 50000.00 5
"e" 1994 "Ford" 10000.00 300.00
"e" 1995 "Dodge" 12000.00 400.00
"e" 1996 "Toyota" 13000.00 500.00
```

We need to "encode" the type information within our database to ensure proper handling—that is why each line starts with a single letter, which indicates the type of data in that record. If we had access to a real object database, there would be a better way to keep track of type information; but since we don't, we have to resort to more primitive methods.

You should notice nothing new in OfeTypebound's type declarations; they are exactly the same as the Car types we used in previous chapters.

The new part comes in our procedure declarations, for instance,

```
PROCEDURE (c: Car) Read*;
```

It almost looks as if we have moved our parameter list, but that isn't exactly what has happened. The (c: Car) in the declaration of the procedure is a special kind of formal parameter known as the *receiver*. The **receiver** indicates the type to which this procedure is bound. That is, this particular procedure Read is bound to type Car. Because of this binding, an instance of Car must always be paired with the call to Read. We use the dot notation to denote this pairing,

```
VAR car: CAR;
...
NEW(car);
car.Read;(* Procedure call using the dot notation *)
```

Just as with record fields declared in the base type, type-bound procedures are also implicitly bound to extended types. This means that procedure Read is also defined for Luxury and Economy. But since the processing for Luxury (and Economy) is slightly different than for Car, we need to redefine Read. So we declare a version of Read specific to type Luxury,

```
PROCEDURE (l: Luxury) Read*;
```

And because it would be nice not to have to completely rewrite the procedure, we have a way to call the version of Read that is bound to Car and let it handle part of the processing. This is known as a **super-call**—a call of the procedure of the same name that is bound to the base type. This is done using the '^' operator,

```
l.Read^;
(* Calls the version of procedure Read that is bound
   to Luxury's base type (i.e., Car) *)
```

In this way, we need define only the processing specific to the extension and reuse what has already been written.

The set of Display procedures follow the same model: common processing is done in the procedure bound to the base type, whereas specific processing is done in the procedure bound to the extended type. This allows us to maximize the use and reuse of what we have written.

Let us examine these type-bound procedures in action. In procedure Do, we examine what type of record is to be read and then create an instance of that type in order to read it.

```
In.String(type);   (* Read the type *)
WHILE In.Done & (recordsRead < LEN(arr) ) DO
   IF type = "l" THEN
      NEW(l);(* New must be called with an appropriate
            argument.  Otherwise,  the  proper  object
            won't be allocated. *)
      c := l
   ELSIF type = "e" THEN
      NEW(e);
      c := e;
   ELSE


   . . .
```

It should be clear why we need to call NEW(l) and NEW(e): NEW needs to be called with a *specific* type of pointer. (Recall that the type of the pointer passed to NEW determines the type of the record that is allocated.) But why do we assign each object to c? The only specific processing is the allocation; after that, all cars undergo the same operations. Cars are read and then displayed; there is no need to explicitly test which type of object is being considered.

Oberon keeps track of the dynamic type for us; any call to Read or Display is correctly resolved at run-time by the current dynamic type of the bound instance. In other words the type-bound call,

```
c.Read;
```

implicitly incorporates a kind of type test. If the dynamic type of c is Luxury, PROCEDURE (l: Luxury) Read is called. If the dynamic type of c is Economy, PROCEDURE (e: Economy) Read is called.

Just as we have seen before, all Cars can be stored in the same array, and now further processing can be done without having to perform type tests.

```
arr[i].Display;
```

will call the appropriate version of Display based on the dynamic type of arr[i].

19.2   Details of Type-bound Procedures

Type-bound procedures in Oberon provide a way to implement an abstract data type with dynamically bound operations. Procedures are connected to a data (object) type explicitly. During run-time, the dynamic type of the instance determines which procedure is called.

The general form of a type-bound procedure declaration is,

```
PROCEDURE (<receiver>) <procedure name> (<parameter list>);
```

The receiver acts as an additional formal parameter to the procedure. The presence of a receiver is an indicator that the procedure is type-bound. The receiver is named and given a type—just like other formal parameters. The receiver must be either a variable parameter of record type, or a value parameter of type pointer to record.

```
PROCEDURE (c: Car) SetYear (y: INTEGER); (* Ok *)

PROCEDURE (VAR c: CarDesc) SetYear (y: INTEGER); (* Ok *)

PROCEDURE (VAR c: Car) SetPrice (p: REAL);
(* ERROR!! Can't be VAR pointer *)

PROCEDURE (c: CarDesc) SetPrice (p: REAL);
(* ERROR!! Need VAR for record *)
```

The declaration of a type-bound procedure makes an explicit binding of the procedure to the receiver's type. The procedure is then implicitly also bound to all extensions. Type-bound procedures are local to their type, just like any other fields of a record. In fact, the browser lists the procedures within the record type declaration,

```
DEFINITION OfeTypebound;

   TYPE
      Car = POINTER TO CarDesc;
      CarDesc = RECORD
         PROCEDURE (c: Car) Display;
         PROCEDURE (c: Car) Read;
      END ;

      Economy = POINTER TO EconomyDesc;

      Luxury = POINTER TO LuxuryDesc;

   PROCEDURE Do;

END OfeTypebound.
```

When types are later extended, additional procedures may then be bound to the extended types. Procedures can also be redefined in extended types. The overridden procedure must have the exact same name and formal parameter list,

```
PROCEDURE (c: Car) SetYear (y: INTEGER);

PROCEDURE (l: Luxury) SetYear (y: REAL);
(* ERROR!!! parameter type mismatch *)
```

Function procedures may also be type-bound. Note that the result type in the redefined function must be identical to the original procedure.

At run-time, the applicable procedure is bound to the dynamic type of the variable (object); this may be a *different procedure* from the one bound to the static type of the variable. The bound variable is passed in a manner similar to that of ordinary arguments via the normal parameter passing rules.

```
PROCEDURE (c: Car) SetYear (y: INTEGER);
BEGIN
    c.year := y (* c can be used just like any other
                    parameter to SetYear *)
END SetYear;
```

Once a type-bound procedure has been redefined by an extended type, the original procedure is effectively hidden. But, we may not want to rewrite the procedure completely, only implement the new behavior and let the original procedure do the rest of the work. Oberon provides the super-call as a way to access the redefined procedure. Using the '^' operator, we can write

```
l.Display^;     (* Calls the procedure bound to l's
                    base type, i.e., Car *)
```

When programming for reuse, it is sufficient to extend the base type and redefine only those type-bound procedures that change. If the procedure already performs as necessary, you aren't required to redefine procedures in extended types,

```
PROCEDURE (l: Luxury) SetYear (y: INTEGER);
(* This procedure is legal, but perfectly useless. *)
BEGIN
    l.SetYear^(y)
END SetYear;
```

There was no need to redefine this procedure; it works fine as declared for Car. In fact, by "layering" the call, it might have been made less efficient (probably requiring two procedure calls instead of one).

Type-bound procedures may be declared even in cases where no action has yet been defined; this is known as an **abstract procedure** declaration. Abstract procedures provide a sort of template for extended types to follow. In this way, a programmer writing an extension knows what needs to be redefined and what its parameters should be. This is a definite advantage when several people are extending the same base type.

It is usually a good idea to call HALT in the body of an abstract procedure; then if the programmer forgets to redefine it, an obvious error occurs.

Because Oberon delegates encapsulation responsibilities to the module rather than the type, it could be considered a disadvantage that all type-bound procedures must be declared in the same module that defines the type itself. However, if types and their primitive operations are carefully designed, this is rarely a serious concern.

19.3   An Object Example: Generic Lists

One of the main goals of extensible design is support for reuse. This means that we want to make procedures and types as *generic* as possible (and likewise, as is sensible to do so). Although some languages provide specific language features for **generic structures**—structures that can be used with many different data types—Oberon relies on type extension (and type-bound procedures) to build generic structures.

Lists, such as we saw in chapter 16 on pointers, are a good candidate for being made generic. Lists are useful in so many different applications, on many different data types, that it seems wasteful to create new list structures every time we need them. Let us examine how lists can be made generic:

```
MODULE OfeGenericLists;
(* To demonstrate the use of generic lists *)

    TYPE
        Item* = POINTER TO ItemDesc;
        (* Items are the objects that make up lists. *)
        ItemDesc* = RECORD
            next: Item;
        END;


        List* = POINTER TO ListDesc;
        (* The type for the list itself. We need to keep track
           of only the first item *)
        ListDesc* = RECORD
            first: Item;
        END;


    PROCEDURE (l: List) Add*(i: Item);
    (* Adds an item to the beginning of the list *)
    BEGIN
        i.next := l.first;
        l.first := i;
```

```
END Add;

PROCEDURE (l: List) Remove*(VAR i: Item);
(* Removes an item from the beginning of the list *)
BEGIN
    IF (l.first # NIL) THEN      (* don't remove an item if
                                    the list is empty *)
        i := l.first;
        l.first := l.first.next;
        i.next := NIL
    ELSE
        i := NIL;
    END;
END Remove;

PROCEDURE (l: List) isEmpty*(): BOOLEAN;
(* Test if the list is empty *)
BEGIN
    RETURN l.first = NIL;
END isEmpty;

PROCEDURE Init*(l: List);
(* Initialize a list *)
BEGIN
    l.first := NIL;
END Init;

END OfeGenericLists.
```

Module OfeGenericLists reimplements, with some slight differences, the list structure we discussed in chapter 16 on pointers. Here, however, the list has been made more generic.

There are two object types declared in OfeGenericLists: List and Item. This is a logical separation of the list itself and the items that go on the list.

There are only four procedures provided for operations on lists: Init, Add, Remove, and isEmpty(). These are the bare minimum for primitive operations for lists. There are a number of other operations that could be provided, but these four are sufficient to constitute a useful list type.

Init sets the pointer to the first element of the list to NIL. That is, it sets the list to empty. Notice that Init is not type-bound. If for some reason we wanted to extend List, we might want to add additional parameters to Init, which isn't possible if it had been made type-bound.

Both Add and Remove operate on the "beginning" or "front" of the list. This is, of course, not the only place where we might wish to add and remove items, but if such functionality were required, other procedures could be added.

The function isEmpty() is provided to allow the implementation of the list to be hidden; then we don't need to know anything about the implementation to test whether the list is empty.

OfeGenericLists does nothing by itself; we need a client module:

```
MODULE OfeListTest;

(* To test the generic list module *)

    IMPORT  Lists := OfeGenericLists, Out;

    (*  Provide  an  alias  for  OfeGenericLists;  it's  a
        relatively long name *)

    TYPE
        IntItem* = POINTER TO IntItemDesc;
        IntItemDesc* = RECORD (Lists.ItemDesc)
        (* Notice we extend the item, not the list *)
            int*: LONGINT;
        END;

    PROCEDURE Do*;
    (* Creates a list and adds some items to it. Then creates
       a second list and moves the items to the second list
       before writing the list of items out to the log *)
        VAR list1, list2: Lists.List; i: LONGINT;
            int : IntItem; item: Lists.Item;
    BEGIN
        NEW(list1); Lists.Init(list1);
        (* Create and initialize the first list *)
        FOR i := 2 TO 20 BY 2 DO
            NEW(int);       (* Create each item *)
            int.int := i;        (* and assign it a value before
                                    adding it to the list *)
            list1.Add(int);
        END; (* FOR *)

        NEW(list2); Lists.Init(list2);
        WHILE (~list1.isEmpty()) DO
            list1.Remove(item);        (*  Notice  the  use  of
                                          'item' and not 'int' *)
            list2.Add(item);
        END; (* WHILE *)
```

```
WHILE (~list2.isEmpty()) DO
    list2.Remove(item);
    Out.Int(item(IntItem).int, 0); Out.Ln
    (* Notice the type-guard *)
END; (* WHILE *)

END Do;
```

```
END OfeListTest.
```

OfeListTest imports OfeGenericLists (using an import alias) and then creates an extended type of Item. The list itself doesn't need to be extended. It can hold any type of Item; that is, Item and its subtypes.

You might want to pay special attention to calls to procedure Remove,

```
list1.Remove(item);
```

We don't remove objects of type IntItem. Look back at the declaration of Remove,

```
PROCEDURE (l: List) Remove*(VAR i: Item);
```

The type of Remove's parameter is Item. As a variable parameter, arguments must have that exact type because the value can be changed. That is, if we tried to invoke Remove as

```
list1.Remove(int);          (* ERROR! *)
```

we would get a compile-time error. The reason is that the list is generic—it can hold any type of Item. The compiler cannot assume that the list holds only IntItems (even though that is all we put on it); so Remove allows removal of only Items.

However, removing objects using item as an argument isn't much of a problem—IntItems are subtypes of Item, so they can usually be handled in the same manner. The only time we need to know the particular subtype is when accessing a field specific to an IntItem. As in the call to Out.Int,

```
Out.Int(item(IntItem).int, 0);
```

All Items don't have an int field, so the type-guard is required. Notice the potential trap waiting to happen—here we assume that the dynamic type of item is IntItem. In this situation, we know for certain that it can be nothing else. Most of the time, it is safer to provide explicit type-tests or use WITH statements. For example,

```
WITH
    item: IntItem DO
        Out.Int(item.int, 0)
ELSE
    Out.String("Unknown type of item on list")
END; (* WITH *)
Out.Ln
```

19.4 Exercises

1. Describe type-bound procedures and explain their benefits.

2. Explain the purpose of a receiver in a type-bound procedure and how it compares to normal parameters.

3. Explain dynamic binding and how it relates to type-bound procedures. Make sure to include an explanation of super-calls.

4. A queue is a structure somewhat similar to a stack, but where elements can be accessed only in a first-in-first-out (FIFO) manner. This means that the first element to be inserted is the only one that can be removed (items are added to the "back" and removed from the "front"). Create a generic Queue type and a related Item type (Item can be extended to hold any sort of data). Write the following type-bound procedures for Queues:

    a. Insert—adds an item to the "back" of the queue.
    b. Remove—removes an item from the "front" of the queue.
    c. NumberOfItems—integer function that returns the current number of items in the queue.
    d. Clear—empties the queue.
    e. IsEmpty—boolean function returning TRUE if the queue is empty.

5. Create a true String object type in which the size of the string can be changed at run-time. Make sure to include all of the functionality that was available in the Strings module from chapter 12. Also, you must include procedures that can convert to and from character arrays. Note that procedures like Append and Insert will resize the String so that no characters are ever lost. Are there any procedures that can be changed to functions that return a String? Are there any procedures that should not be type-bound?

6. Most Oberon compilers come with a module Files to access disk files. Check your compiler to see if such a module is available. Use Files to write a procedure CopyFile, which will copy one file to another. The steps you will have to take will look something like,

    > Open the "old" file.
    > Open the "new" file.
    > While there is data left in the "old" file,
    > Read a byte from the "old" file
    > Write that byte to the "new" file.
    > Close both files. (You may have to "register" the "new" file as well.)

What other procedures does module Files provide? Can you figure out what they all are for?

7. Create a ComplexNumber type that has real and imaginary parts. Write procedures that perform all the operations available for complex numbers. Do you have to write special procedures in order for ComplexNumbers to interact with REALs?

Chapter 20
Additional Topics

20.1   What Else Is There?

If you have ever browsed the shelves in the computer section of your local bookstore, you couldn't possibly have any illusions that this one book would cover all there is to know about programming.

Although this book has attempted to provide comprehensive coverage of the Oberon-2 programming language, it is still an introduction to *programming*. We have discussed simple programming structures and have seen a basic overview of analysis and design. With a firm understanding of these fundamentals, you should be prepared for further study of programming and software development from other sources.

However, a few additional topics may be of interest. Each of these topics could take an entire chapter for a thorough discussion (or even a whole book in some cases); but the following sections at least provide a starting point.

20.2   Exception Handling

An **exception** is a condition that lies outside of normal program operation. The occurrence of exceptions might lead to incorrect results or abnormal program termination. When we provide special processing for exceptional situations, we can say that exceptions are detected by being *raised*, and once detected can be *handled* by the program.

Exception handling allows a system to continue to run, in known states, no matter what happens. Programs that don't do an adequate job of handling exceptions may crash periodically or produce erroneous information. It is the job of the programmer to prevent this from happening. A programmer must continually consider possible exception conditions and how to handle them throughout the design and creation of software.

Exceptions can be encountered at various times:

- Incoming—as input to modules and procedures. This can be data read from files or databases, as user input, or as arguments to procedures. Are the data in an expected format? Are the values in range?

- Outgoing—as output from modules and procedures. Where are data being sent? Can you open the appropriate file? Are the data formatted properly? Are they in the correct type and range of values?
- Result—data are unable to be processed correctly. Perhaps your calculations couldn't be performed; for example, a divide by zero error occurred.
- Status—values are unavailable. Are there flags within a data structure that can be checked? Are there missing data that keeps you from continuing?
- Implementation—limits on structures. Have you reached the end of an array? Are you trying to get data from an empty list?
- System—hardware and operating system limitations. Have you reached some system-specific limitation, say, a disk is full?

Exceptions can also be of varying severity:

- Fatal exception—the program must be halted; the exception is so severe that it can neither be handled nor be ignored.
- Nonpropagating—only the current procedure (or module) is halted. Other processing is not affected.
- Recoverable—the exceptional data can be repaired or ignored safely; the procedure can then continue.

How can exceptions be prevented? Unlike some programming languages, Oberon does not provide special language constructs to handle exceptions. Programmers must test for exception conditions using IF statements and the predeclared procedure ASSERT. Calls to ASSERT should be used to test for fatal and nonpropagating exceptions; at the same time, IF statements can be used for recoverable exceptions (and in some cases, nonpropagating exceptions as well).

Entire books have been written on how to write quality software, so we won't belabor the point here. Just realize that quality programs don't happen by accident. You must be continually vigilant for potentially exceptional situations from the start.

Oberon is generally a "safe" language. Oberon's strong type checking and interface checking catch many potential errors at compile-time. Garbage collection prevents memory deallocation errors at run-time. Oberon also does run-time type checking and other important run-time checks. But programmers are still ultimately responsible for their programs to run correctly.

20.3 Recursion

A procedure that calls itself is recursive, and this self-reference is called **recursion**.

```
PROCEDURE SumDigits*(theNum: LONGINT): LONGINT;
    VAR number: LONGINT;
BEGIN
```

```
    number := theNum MOD 10;
    IF (theNum DIV 10 # 0) THEN
        RETURN number + SumDigits(theNum DIV 10)
                        (* Recursive call! *)
    END; (* IF *)
    RETURN number
END SumDigits;
```

If you recall, procedure calls are usually implemented using a program stack. Each successive call to the recursive procedure creates another copy of the procedure's "environment" on the stack. This consumption of the stack's resources may lead to some potential difficulties.

First, the stack may run out of room (similar to an out-of-memory condition). So a very large number of recursive calls may result in a stack error.

Also, as with any procedure call, copying the procedure's environment to the stack takes a certain amount of time. Even though this period of time is relatively small, with large numbers of procedure calls this could become a source of inefficiency in a program.

Even with these difficulties, recursion is often the most straightforward way to express the solution to a programming problem.

Recursion can be thought of as another type of looping mechanism. In this case, the recursive call *is* the loop. Recursive calls can be translated into the other forms of loops,

```
PROCEDURE SumDigits*(theNum: LONGINT): LONGINT;
(* "Iterative" version of SumDigits. Uses a while loop. *)
    VAR number, total: LONGINT;
BEGIN
    total := 0;
    WHILE (theNum # 0) DO
        number := theNum MOD 10;
        INC(total, number);
        theNum := theNum DIV 10
    END; (* WHILE *)
    RETURN total
END SumDigits;
```

In **tail recursion**, the recursive call is at the end of the procedure, so there are no unfinished statements left after the call. Tail recursion most easily translates into other forms of looping.

Again, as with other loops, be sure to include an exit condition to avoid *infinite recursion*. You should define the exit condition (bound), and write the procedure so that each successive call brings it one step closer to that condition.

Recursion is good for "divide and conquer" type problems. Recursion also provides a way to "backtrack" along list structures without having backward pointers.

20.4 Procedure Types

As with everything in Oberon, procedures have a type associated with them. In the procedures we have declared up to this point, the type is anonymous and the procedure itself is constant. That is, we cannot explicitly change the procedure associated with a particular identifier.

However, we could take the view that procedures are themselves objects that can be assigned to variables.

```
TYPE
    ProcType = PROCEDURE (a: SomeType, b: AnotherType);
    (* procedure type declaration *)

    ObjDesc = RECORD
        proc: ProcType (* field of procedure type *)
    END;


VAR
    p: ProcType; (* variable with procedure type *)
```

A procedure type declaration specifies the number and the types of the formal parameters, and in the case of a function procedure, the type of the result.

The identifiers that appear in the parameter list of the procedure type declaration are really only placeholders. They aren't used during a real procedure call (although they can serve as a mnemonic as to the purpose of each parameter). It is their type that is important.

Procedure types are compatible if their formal parameter lists match. That is,

- They must have the same number of parameters.
- Corresponding parameters must have equal types, and are either both variable parameters or both value parameters.

In the case of function procedures, they must also have the same function result type. Procedure variables can be declared of procedure type.

```
    VAR p, q: ProcType;
```

Procedure variables can be compared for equality or inequality.

```
    IF (p # q) THEN ...
    (* do p and q currently refer to the same procedure? *)
```

Procedure variables can be assigned to using the ':=' operator. "Normal" procedures can be assigned to compatible procedure variables.

```
PROCEDURE NormalProcedure(a: SomeType, b: AnotherType);
BEGIN ... END NormalProcedure;
```

```
p := NormalProcedure;
p(a, b);
(* A procedure call through a procedure variable *)
```

The procedure and the procedure variable must be declared within the same scope. For example, local procedures cannot be assigned to global procedure variables. Predeclared procedures can never be assigned to procedure variables.

NIL is compatible with all procedure types. That is, NIL may be assigned to or compared with all procedure variables. NIL can be used to initialize procedure variables.

```
q := NIL;
...
IF (q # NIL) THEN
    (* A check to be sure that q has been assigned a
    procedure value before calling it *)
        q(a, b);
END (* IF *)
```

A procedure variable may be called; the rules are identical to the call of a normal procedure. Note that an attempt to call a procedure variable whose value is NIL results in a trap. Recall that, as always, function calls must always have parentheses (with a possibly empty argument list).

Parameters can be declared of procedure type,

```
TYPE CompareType = PROCEDURE(x, y: SomeType): INTEGER;

PROCEDURE Sort(c: CompareType; ... )
```

or

```
PROCEDURE Sort(c: PROCEDURE(x, y: SomeType): INTEGER, ... )
```

In this way, different sorting routines can be called depending on the situation. Passing the procedure as a parameter can make it more general-purpose. But because Oberon-2 provides type-bound procedures, most of the time procedure types aren't necessary for conditional processing.

A situation that might lend itself to the use of procedure types is a *coroutine module*. **Coroutines** provide a method for *threading* programs. **Threads** are actions that logically occur at the same time; that is, independent procedures that execute concurrently.

A typical definition module might look like the following:

```
DEFINITION Coroutines;

    TYPE
        Coroutine = RECORD END;
        Body = PROCEDURE;

    PROCEDURE Init (body: Body; VAR cor: Coroutine);
```

```
PROCEDURE Transfer (VAR from, to: Coroutine);
END Coroutines.
```

Init creates and initializes a new coroutine. The name of the procedure to be used as the coroutine's "body" is provided as an argument to Init. In this case, the "body" procedure can be any parameterless procedure that is not predeclared. The initialized coroutine is started by a Transfer to it.

20.5   The SYSTEM Module

Because Oberon is used on a great number of different kinds of computer systems, the module SYSTEM contains procedures necessary to implement low-level operations. Use of the SYSTEM module should be restricted to cases in which these low-level operations are absolutely required because they generally aren't portable to other computer systems.

Although not a proper part of the Oberon language, the SYSTEM module is provided by most Oberon compilers. Procedures are provided for dealing directly with memory addresses and values at the bit level; these can be necessary for accessing devices that are controlled by hardware. SYSTEM also provides a method for "breaking" type compatibility rules.

Any module with SYSTEM appearing in its import list should be considered nonportable.

We won't cover all that the SYSTEM module has to offer here (check your compiler documentation for more details). However, we should note one interesting and potentially important function procedure: VAL() is used to convert from one type to another. This can be very useful when reading data from other computer systems or other programming languages.

VAL() is also often used in conjunction with set variables in order to directly manipulate the bits that comprise, say, an integer value.

```
MODULE OfeVal;

  IMPORT SYSTEM, Out;

  PROCEDURE Union*(a, b: LONGINT): LONGINT;
    VAR s, t: SET;
  BEGIN
    s := SYSTEM.VAL(SET, a);
    t := SYSTEM.VAL(SET, b);
    RETURN SYSTEM.VAL(LONGINT, s + t)
  END Union;

  PROCEDURE Do*;
    VAR x, y: LONGINT;
```

```
BEGIN
    x := 2;
    y := 4;
    x := Union(x, y);
    Out.Int(x, 0); Out.Ln
END Do;

END OfeVal.
```

Procedure Union performs a "bitwise union" (also called a "bitwise and") on the values contained in a and b. This procedure assumes that SIZE(LONGINT) = SIZE(SET), which may or may not be true, depending on your implementation. This makes Union nonportable between Oberon compilers.

Procedures such as Union may be necessary when accessing libraries written in other languages; for instance, you need to set values of individual bits, but the value you are given is of integer type.

One last note: You should never use VAL() to assign a value to a pointer variable. This would in all likelihood cause serious problems for the Oberon garbage collector. The garbage collector needs to be sure of the type of objects for proper deallocation. VAL() corrupts any knowledge about the actual type of an object.

20.6 Exercises

1. Explain the differences between exceptions and errors.

2. Describe the different kinds of exceptions and their levels of severity. Give examples from your own programming work of each kind and how you handled it.

3. Some programming languages provide specific exception-handling features. Can you think of some addition to the Oberon language that might help in handling exceptions? Describe such a feature and what its benefits would be.

4. Describe the advantages and disadvantages of recursion.

5. Write a recursive procedure to calculate the factorial of an integer. The factorial of a number n (the mathematical notation is n!) is $n * (n - 1) * (n - 2) * \ldots * 3 * 2 * 1$. For example, 6! is $6 * 5 * 4 * 3 * 2 * 1 = 720$. What exceptional situations must you watch out for? Write an iterative version of the same procedure.

6. Rewrite the Insert procedure for the Queue type from the exercises in chapter 19 so that it is recursive.

7. Type-bound procedures can, in many cases, be used rather than procedure types. What are the advantages and disadvantages of using procedure types instead of type-bound procedures?

8. Reimplement the Queue type from chapter 19 so that it uses procedure types (and procedure variables) rather than type-bound procedures.

9. Examine the SYSTEM module for your compiler. Explain why each of the facilities you find is system dependent. Is there anything in SYSTEM that you feel could have been included in the Oberon language? Explain your answer.

References

Books:

Programming in Oberon—Steps Beyond Pascal and Modula
Martin Reiser, Niklaus Wirth
New York: Addison-Wesley, 1992 (ISBN 0-201-56543-9)

Oh my! Modula-2!
Doug Cooper.
New York: Norton, 1990 (ISBN 0-393-96009-9)

Papers:

The Programming Language Oberon-2
H. Mössenböck, N. Wirth
Structured Programming, Vol.12, No.4, 1991

From Modula to Oberon
Niklaus Wirth
Software Practice and Experience Vol. 18, No. 7, July 1988

Object-Oriented Programming in Oberon-2
H. Mössenböck
Proceedings of the Second International Modula-2 Conference,
Loughborough, September 1991